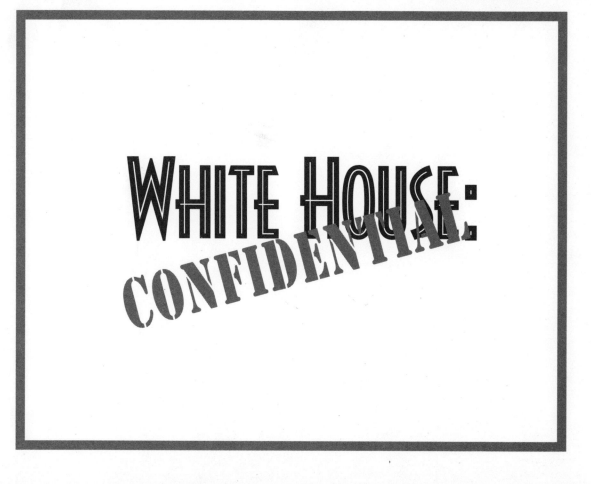

WHITE HOUSE: CONFIDENTIAL

The Little Book of Weird Presidential History

GREGG STEBBEN & JIM MORRIS

CUMBERLAND HOUSE PUBLISHING

Nashville, Tennessee

Published by Cumberland House Publishing, Inc., 431 Harding Industrial Drive, Nashville, TN 37211.

Cover and interior design by Gore Studios, Inc.

Typesetting by Leslie Peterson.

Library of Congress Cataloging-in-Publication Data

Stebben, Gregg, 1961-

    White House confidential : the little book of weird Presidential values / Gregg Stebben & Jim Morris.

       p. cm.

    ISBN 1-888952-68-7 (pbk. : alk. paper)

    1. Presidents—Unites States—History—Miscellanea.

  2. Presidents—United States—Biography—Miscellanea. I. Morris, Jim, 1957- . II. Title.

  E176.1.S7 1998

973'.09'9—cd21   98-9755

                                                      CIP

Printed in the United States of America

1 2 3 4 5 6 7—04 03 02 01 00 99 98

FOR OUR MOTHERS, ARLENE AND MARILYN:

You may not have raised us to be presidents . . .
but you did at least teach us right from wrong.

AND FOR OUR WIVES, JODY AND KATHY,

who taught us all the rest.

Contents

INTRODUCTION

PRESIDENT OF THE UNITED STATES. What a rotten job.

You're the guy or gal who's always to blame. The economy. Foreign policy. Drugs in the schools. Crime on the streets. . . . It's all your fault.

Throw in the official duties: commander in chief of the armed services and chief executive of the biggest, fattest, least efficient organization in the known world. You've got the power to nominate your good friends A, B, and C for secretary of state, Supreme Court justice, or maybe ambassador to some country called Paradíso. But you've got to do it without ticking off the general public, too many members of Congress, or your good friends X, Y, and Z (who thought they were going to get the jobs because that's what you said you were going to do). You also get the power to declare war. (Yikes! What if you do it and in retrospect realize you were just having a bad day?) And on top of all that you've got to decide whether you should sign or veto a bunch of bills from Congress—and every time you try to read one you fall fast asleep.

All of which causes you to wonder: Does anyone—other than your press secretary, a handful of radio call-in talk show hosts, and a couple of other people with political futures at stake—really care about any of this stuff?

Somehow you get the sense that what the American public really expects from you, their president, is entertainment. Giant, screaming headlines full of corruption, scandal, sex, stupidity, sleaze. And presumably they want that sex, stupidity, and sleaze to be yours. After all, you've finally made it. You're in the center ring. You're president of the United States—the all-star attraction. And now it's you everyone wants as the fall guy.

This of course means that it's also your job to collaborate with the media to destroy your life, your reputation, your family and your knees (a reference to tumbling, tumbling Gerald Ford and Bill Clinton, as well as to Thomas Jefferson, who once took a spill while showing off for his married girlfriend), all in an effort to entertain the American people.

Thus far, our legion of presidents have lived up to the challenge. And when there's been nothing true to report, the media has been only too happy to help out; in the absence of truth they report on rumor, innuendo, a thread of a thread of a story heard somehow, somewhere.

Are we, the people, really this callous? Petty? Shallow? Or easily amused?

Probably not.

The truth is most of us would rather have a straight-shooting, stand-up kind of president than one who's a buffoon or a scoundrel or a cheat. In fact, what most of us really want is a president who's a hero. Or a saint. Someone with impeccable moral values and judgment. A flawless personal history. The sort of guy or gal who has never made an enemy or, barring that, the sort who has made many—but for all the right, fight-for-what-you-believe-in reasons.

Yup. This is what we desperately crave, even though it's a standard we ourselves could never hope to live up to. So we take what we can get, and then we act horrified when our presidents and presidential candidates do the same dirty, rotten stuff with their lives we do with ours.

And now that you've spent the last few moments imagining the job was yours, aren't you relieved to remember it's a job that actually belongs to someone else?

A couple of small disclaimers

I. Your authors, too, are members of the media. Therefore we want to fulfill our obligation to you, the reader, by entertaining you with stories about the presidents based either on the stupid, rotten stuff they've actually done or at least the stupid, rotten stuff of which they've been publically accused. However, we want to do this without creating a scandal of our own. For that reason we state up front that this work contains absolutely no groundbreaking or earth-shattering new research on the behavior of presidents past or present. Furthermore, we makes absolutely no warrants toward the truth or veracity of any of the information contained in this book.

This much you can count on, however: If it appears here, regardless of how cruel, mean, baseless, or untrue it may be, someone somewhere (other than your authors) reported it first.

II. Much of what you read in this book is funny today, but it wasn't very funny when it happened. Why not? For the same reason you're probably not laughing about the Savings and Loan debacle or Watergate or Contragate or Whitewater. History is rarely entertaining for those who are deceived or wronged or maligned or misled or screwed in the course of the history-making process. For this reason, you'll find many more juicy tidbits about presidents of the first hundred and seventy or so years of our history than about our past five or six commanders in chief. After all, we're the ones who have to ante up for their follies, and that's no laughing matter.

WEIRD FAMILY VALUES!

HOW'S THIS FOR WEIRD:

Franklin Delano *Roosevelt* married
his fifth cousin, Eleanor *Roosevelt.*
At the wedding Eleanor was given away
by her uncle—Theodore *Roosevelt,*
president of the United States.

With FDR and Eleanor though . . .

THIS WAS JUST THE BEGINNING of a lifetime of weirdness that involved mistresses, lesbians, and live-in lovers right there at the White House!

Most people would agree that the best way to avoid getting caught when having an affair is to have it with someone your spouse doesn't know. Guess no one told FDR that—his first mistress was Lucy Mercer, Eleanor's social secretary.

When Eleanor found out FDR was having an affair, she offered to let him out of their marriage. But FDR didn't take her up on it; he knew Lucy, being Catholic, would never marry a man who was divorced. Oh, and there might have been one other small reason why FDR didn't want to divorce Eleanor: He knew that if he did his mother would cut him off from the family fortune.

After he and Lucy got caught, FDR had to find a new mistress. *Hey, I've got a great idea!* he might have thought to himself, *Maybe I'll go look for one down in the secretarial pool!* But you can't say he didn't learn from experience—instead of having an affair with Mrs. Roosevelt's new secretary, he had his next affair with a new secretary of his own.

Her name was Missy LeHand, and everyone in the Roosevelt family—Eleanor and all six kids—knew about the relationship. Of course, it would have been impossible for them not to know—Missy was living with the president right there at the White House.

Obviously the president and Missy had to show some decorum. That's why Missy had her own set of rooms—a living room, bedroom, and bath—at the White House, although she could frequently be seen sitting on the president's lap in the Oval Office at night or in her bathrobe in the president's own suite. Lady that she was, however, she was always gone by breakfast.

In the meantime, Eleanor embarked on a strange, "secret" life of her own that first

Lovers?
Or just very
good friends?

★ ★ ★

Some have said that Eleanor's attachment to strong women like Lorena Hickok was emotional but not physical. Following is a letter Eleanor sent to Hick in 1933—you be the judge:

Good-night, dear one. I want to put my arms around you and kiss you at the corner of your mouth. And in a little more than a week now—I shall.

involved a rough-hewn, cigar-chomping reporter from the Associated Press. Lorena Hickok was her name, and she and Eleanor were lovers (spiritually, if not physically) for more than ten years.

Eleanor and "Hick," as Lorena was often called, had their own bizarre living arrangements at the White House. The two women had separate rooms across the West Hall and could often be seen running back and forth from one another's quarters.

Eleanor was a good sport about FDR's living arrangements with Missy—after all, it had been going on since he was governor of New York. On the other hand, the president wasn't so crazy about having Hick hanging around. One day, he stormed through the White House yelling, "I want that woman kept out of this house!" From that point on, the White House maids and Eleanor did everything they could to keep the president and Hick apart.

The weird story of the Roosevelts has

Oh, Happy Day!

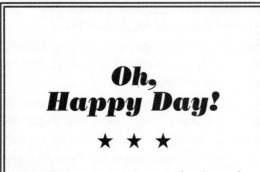

★ ★ ★

FDR's first Inauguration Day, that is. And why shouldn't it have been happy? After all, FDR knew his wife would be there. And he knew that his lover, Missy LeHand, would be there. And he knew (but kept it secret from both Eleanor and Missy) that his former lover, Lucy, would be there too. Not that Eleanor would have noticed—after all, she spent the night before the inauguration at a hotel with Hick and, like a young schoolgirl in love, wore Hick's sapphire ring on her finger as she attended the festivities of the day.

many endings, by the way—but not all of them are happy:

- While living at the White House with Eleanor, Lorena Hickok fell in love with another woman and moved out.
- Missy LeHand suffered a cerebral hemorrhage, had to be hospitalized, and then died.
- Shortly after Missy fell ill, the husband of FDR's old flame, Lucy Mercer, had a devastating stroke, so she and FDR "took up" again.
- It was Lucy Mercer, not Eleanor, who was with FDR when he died of a stroke in 1945.
- Perhaps, in these cases, money speaks louder than words. When FDR died his estate was worth an estimated $1.9 million. He left half of that to his wife, Eleanor, and the other half to cover Missy LeHand's medical bills. There wasn't a cent left over for Lucy Mercer.

Did FDR treat his dog better than his wife?

★ ★ ★

Fala was a little Scotch terrier FDR took with him everywhere (although he certainly didn't extend the same invitation to Eleanor). To the press and public Fala was known as "The Informer" because wherever FDR traveled—even if his plans were secret because of the war—Fala had to be walked at every train stop and thus gave the president's "secret" presence away.

LET'S TAKE A LOOK AT ANOTHER ROOSEVELT

Teddy Roosevelt's wife, Alice, and his mother both died on the same day: January 14, 1884. His mother died of typhoid; his wife died of Bright's disease three days after giving birth to daughter Alice.

Three years later Teddy married an old childhood friend, Edith. Together they had five children.

Unlike his naughty nephew, Teddy didn't feel a need to run wild. Instead he was a devoted family man. Yet the Teddy Roosevelt White House was almost as much a zoo as FDR's White House because Teddy got great joy from indulging his children's every whim:

- Teddy allowed his kids to keep a few pets, including ten dogs named Susan, Skip, Scamp, Sailor Boy, Peter, Manchu,

Allen, Gem, Jessie, and Bill; a horned toad named Bill; four guinea pigs named Bob Evans, Father Grady, Dewey Jr., and Dewey Sr.; a blue macaw named Eli Yale; Emily Spinach, a garter snake; two ponies named Algonquin and Fidelity; a badger named Josiah; two cats named Tom Quartz and Slippers; a bear named Jonathon Edward; a lion; and a one-legged rooster.

- Every member of Teddy's family owned a pair of stilts—and that included the First Lady. Edith Roosevelt was so well coordinated and so good at playing different games and sports that young Quentin once said of her, "I'll bet Mother was a boy when she was little."
- Once, when Archie Roosevelt was sick in bed with the measles, Teddy saw nothing wrong with letting sons Kermit and Quentin sneak Algonquin the pony up the White House elevator to visit him.
- Daughter Ethel Roosevelt was a notorious tomboy; one of her favorite things to do was to sit on cookie sheets and slide down the White House steps.
- After daughter Alice interrupted one of his meetings at the White House one day, Teddy threw up his arms in resignation and swore, "I can be president of the United States, or I can control Alice. I cannot possibly do both."

Think President Clinton has a "Hillary problem"?

The wife of President John Adams
(the second president of the United States)
had so much influence on her
husband during his term in office
from 1797 to 1801 that most
people referred to her as
"Mrs. President."

"I've committed adultery in my heart. . . ."

—Jimmy Carter,
in an interview with *Playboy* magazine

"Dan Quayle would rather play golf than have sex any day!"

—Marilyn Quayle

Jefferson's Legacy

Whether lusting inside one's heart, or lusting inside the White House, it didn't begin with Jimmy Carter. In fact, Thomas Jefferson—the man who is called our greatest president by many—was also the first to face charges of sexual misconduct.

P.S. Many historians now agree that Jefferson was the father of several illegitimate children.

IT'S THE STRANGE CASE OF THOMAS JEFFERSON

**Was he a devoted and faithful husband?
Or the kind of guy who likes to mess around
with married women and young girls?**

The Thomas Jefferson Story, Part One

In the beginning there was Betsey Walker. She was pretty and vivacious, and she was also married to Thomas Jefferson's good friend, William George Walker.

Jefferson was such a good friend of the bride and groom the couple asked Jefferson to be a member of their wedding party. Not only that, but Thomas Jefferson was such a trusted confidant and buddy to William George that when it was time for him to name an executor of his will, Thomas Jefferson was William George's choice.

But then things went awry—terribly awry. On the eve of leaving town for four months to help negotiate a treaty with the Indians at Fort Stanwix, William George took his good friend and neighbor and the executor of his will aside and asked him to keep an eye on his wife while he was gone. Little did he know that Jefferson actually had the hots for his wife and would strike while the mouse was away, so to speak.

Only years later as the Walkers were rewriting their wills did William George learn of Jefferson's seduction of his wife; it happened when he told Betsey he intended to keep Jefferson as the executor of his will. She was appalled and told him of the incidences from years ago.

The Thomas Jefferson Story, Part Two

At the age of twenty-eight, Thomas Jefferson married Martha Skelton. Jefferson was a loving and adoring husband, and some say Martha was the love of his life.

The problem is Martha and Thomas were only married for ten years. Then Martha died.

No one has ever suggested that Jefferson cheated on his wife. In fact, when Martha asked him, while on her deathbed, to promise never to marry again, he promised and kept his word for the rest of his life.

The Thomas Jefferson Story, Part Three

For four years Jefferson played the role of the widower—no doubt wearing black for a while, then slowly working his way back into a normal life.

Jefferson was only thirty-nine when Martha died, so we can assume every widow within two hundred miles plied him with casseroles and offers of company and more. He never promised Martha he would abstain from sex, after all.

By 1785, five years before he was elected president, Jefferson was living in Paris and serving as U.S. minister to France.

While attending a party, Jefferson met—and fell in love with—the wife of another man. Her name was Maria Cosway, and by all accounts she was a stunning blonde with a coquettish Italian accent, deep blue eyes, curly locks, and a darling cupid's face.

But let's not be sexist here—the attraction wasn't purely physical. She also charmed the socks off Jefferson intellectually. She was a respected painter. She had a beautiful voice and loved to sing. She was a talented harpsichord player. She was a brilliant conversationalist.

As long as Jefferson remained at the party, he found it difficult to leave her side—even though her husband, the renowned Italian painter Richard Cosway, was just on the other side of the room. To prolong the time he could spend in her company, he sent word to the Duchesse de la Rochefoucauld d'Anville, with whom he had dinner plans, that he would need to cancel their previously arranged date.

Jefferson spent the next eight weeks in the constant company of Maria Cosway. Her husband didn't seem to mind. In fact, he seemed to encourage the affair and often left them alone.

When it was time for the Cosways to return to London, Thomas and Maria made plans to meet in Paris again—this time without Maria's husband in tow. Yet when Maria arrived alone the following August as planned, Jefferson—as we say today—blew her off.

The Thomas Jefferson Story, Part Four

Over the years there has been much speculation as to why Jefferson would turn a cold shoulder to the woman who sparked such an intense reaction of love in him the year before. One theory—and our favorite—is that by the time Maria showed up for their next rendezvous he had already taken up with his next paramour.

What woman on earth could replace the beautiful, graceful, and charming Maria Cosway?

One would guess that she might be as young or younger. Probably even more beautiful. And wouldn't you think she'd have to be someone who was more accessible?

Sally Hemings was all of those things and more—she was Jefferson's slave. And even more, she was the half sister of Jefferson's dead wife.

Weird Family Values!

Thomas Jefferson and Sally Hemings were together for thirty-eight years (including Jefferson's eight years as president). Together they were the parents of more than five children.

The Jefferson Addendum

Let's get this straight: Thomas Jefferson as a forty-eight-year-old man took as his lover a seventeen-year-old girl—who happened to be his slave as well as the half sister of his dead wife?

Sounds impossible, but it's true. Jefferson's wife, Martha Skelton, was the daughter of John Wayles. When John Wayles's third wife died he took Betty Hemings, a slave, as his concubine, and they had six children, one of whom was Sally. When John Wayles died, he willed the slave children (including Sally) to his daughter Martha and her husband, Thom.

★ ★ ★

If you want to get technical, Jefferson's idea of a normal life ended when Martha became sick. That's when he resigned from Congress to take care of her. Then, only eight weeks after she died, Jefferson let his friends in government know he was ready to return to the political arena. For that reason, there are those who say that if Martha had lived longer Jefferson wouldn't have returned to Washington so soon, and he might never have become our third president.

"Mrs. Who?"

When Martin Van Buren wrote his autobiography
after serving as president from 1837 to 1841,
he failed to mention his wife of twelve years.
Not even once.

For what it's worth, Van Buren probably
didn't mention his father either. But there was
a rumor floating around during the mid-1800s
that President Martin Van Buren was the illegitimate
son of former Vice President (and traitor and murderer,
but we'll get to that later) Aaron Burr.

DOES SEX SAVE LIVES?

Ben Franklin probably thought so; he was keeping mistresses well past his seventieth birthday—when the average guy might have considered himself lucky to see sixty.

Granted, Ben was never president of the United States, but as one of our Founding Fathers and as a guy who was supposed to be setting an example for his fellow countrymen, his exploits are too good to pass up.

First, there's the story of Ben and Deborah Read. Ben loved Deborah so much that he wanted to marry her. But according to the law he couldn't: A woman who had been married once and then abandoned (as opposed to being divorced or widowed) couldn't get married again.

The punishment for violating this law was pretty stiff: thirty-nine lashes at the public whipping post and a sentence of hard labor for life. So Ben did the next best thing. He asked Deborah to move in and live with him in sin.

Six months later Ben did something even more outrageous: He brought home a son he'd fathered by another woman. On top of that, he took in his new son's mother so she could be closer to their child. So there were Ben and Deborah and the new baby and the new baby's mom—all living in one house.

Weird family values . . . but they didn't seem to hurt the boy. His name was William Franklin, and he went on to be the governor of New Jersey.

Ben didn't seem to feel any shame about his sexuality either. In fact, he took great pleasure in writing about it. In the essay below he explains why, given the choice, he always prefers an older mistress over a younger one:

1. Because as they have more Knowledge of the World and their Minds are better stor'd with Observations, their Conversation is more improving and more lastingly agreeable.
2. Because when Women cease to be handsome, they study to be good. To maintain their Influence over Men, they supply the Diminution of Beauty by an Augmentation of Utility. They learn to do 1000 Services small and great and are the most tender and useful of all Friends when you are sick. Thus they continue amiable. And hence there is hardly such a thing to be found as an old Woman who is not a good Woman.
3. Because there is no hazard of Children, which irregularly produc'd may be attended with much Inconvenience.
4. Because thro' more Experience, they are more prudent and discreet in conducting an Intrigue to prevent Suspicion. The commerce with them is therefore safer with regard to your Reputation. And with regard to theirs, if the Affair should happen to be known, considerate People might be rather inclin'd to excuse an old Woman who would kindly take care of a young Man, form his Manners by her good Counsels, and prevent his ruining his Health and Fortune among mercenary Prostitutes.
5. Because in every Animal that walks upright, the Deficiency of the Fluids that fill the Muscles appears first in the highest Part: The Face first grows land and wrinkled; then the Neck, then the Breast, and regarding only what is below the Girdle, it is impossible of two Women to know an old from a young one. And as in the dark all Cats are grey, the Pleasure of corporal Enjoyment with an old Woman is at least equal, and frequently superior, every Knack being by Practice capable of Improvement.

6. Because the Sin is less. The debauching a Virgin may be her Ruin, and make her Life unhappy.

7. Because the Compunction is less. The having made a young Girl miserable may give you frequent bitter Reflections; none of which can attend the making an old Woman happy.

8. [thly and Lastly] They are so grateful! Thus much for my Paradox. But still I advise you to marry directly.

Meet the hermit of 1600 Pennsylvania Avenue.

★ ★ ★

Her name was Margaret Taylor. She was Zachary Taylor's wife.

All the time she lived at the White House she hid herself out of sight.

She didn't like all the pomp and circumstance—she said—but this is more likely true:

Ol' Margaret preferred smoking her corncob pipe to talking to the likes of you.

Can you name the president?

Who once lived with his wife in an
apartment so small they had to share
a bathroom with the prostitute
down the hall?

A. Gerald Ford
B. George Bush
C. Abraham Lincoln
D. Andrew Jackson
E. All of the above

Answer on page 28.

HERE'S WHAT A FEW OF OUR PAST PRESIDENTS LOOKED FOR IN A WIFE

- **W**hen Ulysses S. Grant met Julia Dent, the first thing he noticed was that her eyes were crossed. He fell in love immediately and proposed marriage on the spot.
- Harry Truman met and fell in love with his wife, Bess, when he was six years old. The attraction? She was the only girl in town who could whistle through her teeth.
- While a young senator, JFK once described what he wanted in a wife to a newspaper reporter: "Intelligent, but not too brainy."

AND WHAT ONE FIRST LADY SAW EVEN THOUGH SHE WASN'T LOOKING

In the years before she was married, Grace Goodhue was a teacher at an institute for the deaf. While watering the school's garden one day, she looked up and saw a man, wearing only a hat and long underwear, standing in front of a mirror in a nearby boarding house. Surprised by this sight, she let out a laugh.

"He heard me and turned to look at me," Grace later recalled. "When he learned who I was, he managed to arrange a formal introduction—and that is how I became Mrs. Calvin Coolidge."

"Fathers" of Our Country?

George Washington is often called
"The Father of His Country" even though
he never had any children.

★ ★ ★

For what it's worth, James Madison is
often called "The Father of the Constitution,"
but he didn't have any kids either.

★ ★ ★

It's also worth noting that Andrew Jackson
raised eleven kids in his lifetime.
None of them were his.

BRATS!

- *T*eddy Roosevelt's son Quentin had his own gang: "The White House Gang." Together, he and his friends did things like drop snowballs off the roof of the White House onto patrolling policemen and throw spitballs at the portraits of earlier presidents.
- Secretary of War Edwin Stanton invented a make-believe military post for his boss Abe Lincoln's son Tad and outfitted the boy with his own Union Army uniform and sword. Being a lieutenant, Tad took it upon himself to order additional weapons for the servants, to march the White House guards and other staff members around, and to dismiss guards who weren't performing to his expectations.
- Jesse Grant, Ulysses S. Grant's son, became interested in stamp collecting and ordered some stamps from a mail-order catalog. When the stamps didn't arrive he convinced Kelly, one of the Capitol policemen, to write a letter. "I am a Capitol policeman," Kelly wrote. "I can arrest anybody, anywhere, at any time, for anything. I want you to send those stamps to Jesse Grant. Kelly, Capitol policeman." Jesse's stamps arrived shortly afterward. Jesse also convinced American ambassadors overseas to send him stamps from the countries in which they were stationed. But his interest in stamp collecting waned when his mother made him send thank-you notes to everyone who sent him stamps.
- JFK and Jackie Kennedy hated TV and had all the televisions taken away from the White House when they moved in . . . until Caroline started to cry when it was time for *Lassie* to come on and they had to have one of the White House servants bring one of the televisions back.

OLDER BRATS!

• **A**ll three of John Quincy Adams's sons fell in love with the same girl, and she was pretty taken with at least two of them herself. First she got engaged to the middle son, George. Then she married the oldest son, John. George and Charles Francis, the youngest, were pretty steamed at her and refused to attend the wedding. To her credit, the bride did what she could for her two brothers-in-law to make up for her past indiscretions—she named a daughter Georgiana Frances after both of them.

• John Tyler had more kids than any other president—eight by his first wife and seven by his second. He was seventy when the last child, Pearl, was born. He was the first president to get married while in office, but his eight kids from his first wife (who had died) did not approve of the union and refused to attend the wedding.

Perhaps his kids objected to how they met.

★ ★ ★

John Tyler was entertaining aboard a naval gunship when a cannon exploded and killed three of his guests, including his secretary of state, his secretary of the navy, and New York senator David Gardiner.

Among the remaining guests was Senator Gardiner's young daughter, Julia. When she heard of her father's death, she fainted into the president's arms. He fell in love and four months later the fifty-four-year-old Tyler and the twenty-four-year-old Julia Gardiner were married.

GROVER CLEVELAND'S LOVE-CHILD-OF-THE-MONTH CLUB

Grover Cleveland's Love Child #1

*F*irst, let's define some terminology: A love child is a child who is conceived out of wedlock. Not such an uncommon thing today, but terribly uncommon in 1884 when Grover Cleveland was running for president.

He was running quite a campaign, too, with a very strong lead over his opponent, until the *Buffalo Evening Telegraph* announced in huge, screaming type he was the father of an illegitimate son.

So Grover Cleveland did what no sane politician has ever done since, given similar circumstances: He told the truth.

He didn't deny the charges. He didn't try to cover his back. He didn't demand a blood test, and he didn't claim he hadn't inhaled, so to speak.

Grover's Truth

*I*n 1871, while sheriff of Buffalo, New York, he met a nice woman named Maria Halpin. He liked her. She liked him. Next thing you know, she was in the family way.

It's important to remember that Cleveland was a bachelor when he was dating Maria Halpin—but the same couldn't be said for the other men she was seeing concurrently, any of which could have been the father.

When Maria came to him with her sad story and demanded that she marry her, he said "No, thank you" but did the next best thing: He offered to provide financial support for the child even though there was a good chance it wasn't his. And he didn't just send money but took an active hand in watching out for the boy's best interests. In fact, at one point when Maria began drinking heavily, Cleveland arranged for her to be institutionalized and for the boy to be adopted by a well-to-do family in New York.

The more the press (and the public) learned about Grover and the honorable way in which he had handled his relationship with Maria Halpin and the boy, the better he looked.

Grover Cleveland's Love Child #2 (Sort Of)

Next thing you know, the newspaper headlines were screaming about another love child. Only this time the love child belonged to Cleveland's opponent, James Blaine.

Turns out Mrs. Blaine gave birth to Junior Blaine only three months after Mr. and Mrs. Blaine were married. That would make Junior love child number two, wouldn't it?

Grover Does It Again

If Grover Cleveland had had his way, no one would ever have known that James Blaine's child was born out of wedlock. In fact, the same informer who leaked the story to the press brought it to Cleveland first. Cleveland read the report, paid the informer, then tore up and burned the evidence. "The other side can have a monopoly on all the dirt," he announced to his shocked and disappointed aides.

Blaine might have learned something from Cleveland about how to deal with the press—but he didn't. Instead of telling the truth, Blaine tried to lie his way out of the story. But lying didn't cut it with the press or the public, and Grover came out ahead at the polls.

Grover Cleveland's Love Child #3

The president didn't conceive this love child either—he married her.

Her name was Frances Folsom. She was the daughter of Cleveland's law partner, and she used to call him "Uncle Cleve." Frances was six when her father died and Cleveland became her legal guardian.

Fifteen years later, at the ages of forty-nine and twenty-one respectively, President Grover Cleveland and Frances Folsom were married.

Grover Cleveland's Love Child #4

Her name was Ruth. She was the very legitimate daughter of President Cleveland and his wife, Frances.

Unlike the other love children in Grover Cleveland's life, there was nothing scandalous about her—except that Nestle's named a candy bar after her and then kept the White House refrigerator and cabinets well stocked with food. Ruth's father, the president, whether contractually obligated to do so or not, ended every public appearance he made by saying, "A Ruth in every pot!"

America loved Baby Ruth. Visitors to the White House would find her playing on the lawn and pick her up and pass her around, excited to have had the chance to see her, touch her.

One day, however, little Ruth stopped going out to play on the lawn. Quickly, rumors spread that she was sick and being hidden from view. A few years later, the rumors proved to be true: Baby Ruth died of cerebral palsy at the age of thirteen.

Answer: George Bush

2

SEX!

*E*VER NOTICE THERE'S A BIG DIFFERENCE between the sex you see in the movies and the sex you have when you get back home? Turns out that with presidents, the same principle applies.

Movie presidents are usually played by guys like Michael Douglas and Harrison Ford. With a few exceptions, real-life presidents usually have about as much sex appeal as, well, Ronald Reagan. George Bush. Gerald Ford. Richard Nixon. Democratic presidents these days tend to be a little younger, so they also tend to be a little sexier . . . but sexy is kind of relative. After all, with the exception of JFK, we're still talking about guys who look like Bill Clinton and Jimmy Carter.

But presidents get girls, there's no doubt about that.

Occasionally a president or president-to-be will marry and stay faithful to his wife—and, for our purposes, that's the end of that. Other times, they marry one woman and still get others. Or they mess around with women who happen to already be married to someone else.

A Few Good (Looking) Men

★ ★ ★

Even Republicans can be good-looking—if you catch them while they're young.

Take Gerald Ford, for example. He appeared on the covers of *Cosmopolitan* and *Look* magazines as a model in the 1930s. And Ronald Reagan won the Most Nearly Perfect Male Figure award from the University of California in 1940.

Sometimes these little indiscretions occur before a president becomes president—but we don't care. Once a president, always a president—even if you're not president yet. Part of acting presidential is to live your life as an open book, allowing the winds of curiosity to blow through the pages for the world to see and browse and judge.

Presidential affairs come in a variety of sizes. Some presidents have wee little affairs, so small and insignificant they're barely worth noticing and hardly worth caring about (unless you're the First Lady, of course). Others have bold, brash, obnoxious affairs that involve a troika of ultimate sins—which is to say they have sex with women other than their wives and they do it in such a way so as to ensure that everyone will know about it and they act as if they don't care who (that's you and us and the First Lady and the media) finds out.

PRESIDENTIAL ADULTERY CHART

PRESIDENT: George Washington

CHEATED ON WHOM: Martha Custis, his fiancée

CHEATED WITH WHO: Sally Fairfax

THE SCOOP: **Did George Washington cheat on Martha?**
He was tall and broad and handsome. He had a successful career and had inherited a small farm. He was polite and soft-spoken. Yet he courted and wooed a number of women, and none wanted anything to do with him. At one point things got so bad for George Washington in the romance department that, after moping around for a while like a lovesick pup, he finally accepted that he would never find a woman to love.

A large part of the problem was that he was already in love. Her name was Sally Fairfax—and she toyed with him and flirted with him and made him feel all light and giddy and gay.

Finally! A woman who would fawn over him and treat him like he was special. Finally! A woman who would respond to his notes of love. Finally! A woman to visit and make love with whenever he could get away from his duties on the front lines of the French and Indian War, where he was commander in chief of the Virginia militia.

Oh, but there were a few minor problems with the relation-

31

ship: For one thing, Sally was married—to one of George's closest friends, George William Fairfax. And if that wasn't bad enough, the two Georges were practically family because George Washington's half brother Lawrence was married to George William's sister Anne.

In spite of all this, George and Sally carried on for as long as seven years—even after George decided that if he couldn't marry for love he would at least marry for money and then got engaged to the richest widow in Virginia, Martha Custis.

Some historians say the relationship between George and Sally never amounted to anything more than a long-term flirtation. Others paint a picture of George riding from battle directly to the home of his love—Sally, not Martha—on those nights while her husband was away. Most historians agree, however, that once married George took his duties as a husband very seriously and what physical relationship he had with Sally ended.

Did George Washington cheat on Martha? Obviously that would depend on which version of history you believe and how you define adultery.

Sex!

"My children may be assured that no illegitimate brother
or sister exists or ever existed."

—JOHN ADAMS

PRESIDENT: John Adams

THE SCOOP: In case you thought sexual liberation and freedom were invented in the sixties, consider this quote from John Adams:

> *No father, brother, son, or friend ever had cause of grief or resentment for any intercourse between me and any daughter, sister, mother, or any other relation with the female sex. My children may be assured that no illegitimate brother exists or ever existed.*

Implied in this statement, of course, is that while Adams stood by watching, everyone else was doing the wild thing with everyone else—and, given what you are about to read in this chart, he was quite right to speak out about his chasteness.

For all his prudishness, Adams was not without a sense of humor. In fact, when Adams heard of a rumor that accused him of dispatching General Charles Cotesworth Pickney to England with a U.S. battleship to pick up four pretty girls so he and the general could each keep two as mistresses, Adams replied to a friend: "If this be true, General Pickney has kept them all for himself and cheated me out of my two!"

PRESIDENT: **Thomas Jefferson**

THE SCOOP: In spite of all his sins, he never committed adultery.

PRESIDENTS: **John Quincy Adams, James Madison, James Monroe**

THE SCOOP: Nope.

PRESIDENT:	**Andrew Jackson**
CHEATED ON WHOM:	**His wife, Rachel**
CHEATED WITH WHOM:	**His wife, Rachel**

THE SCOOP: **Every time this president had sex with his wife, he helped her commit adultery again**

Confused? You should be.

Here's what happened: In 1791 Andrew Jackson married Rachel Donelson Robards—or at least he thought he did.

He first met Rachel when he moved into her family's boarding house as a young attorney, and he was taken with her at first sight. Unfortunately for Jackson, Rachel was married. In fact, she was not only married but was married to a man who was given to insane fits of jealous rage.

This was unfortunate for Jackson—who was an honorable guy—because he really liked Rachel and wanted to be her friend. Unfortunately Rachel's husband, Captain Lewis Robards, perceived Jackson's overtures of friendship as a threat and flew into such a fit that Rachel had to send word home to her family for help. It was Andrew Jackson who went to her rescue and moved her to the safety of her sister's house in Tennessee.

Through word of mouth Jackson heard that Captain Robards had sought and received a divorce from Rachel in his home state of Kentucky. Very much in love, Jackson quickly approached Rachel's mother and asked for her hand in marriage.

Unfortunately, Jackson was so excited at the prospect of marrying the only woman he had ever loved that he neglected to check the veracity of the secondhand report; in reality Captain Robards's divorce from Rachel was not complete. Therefore, for the first two years of their marriage—until Jackson and Rachel took another marriage vow—Rachel was guilty of adultery with her not-legal husband, Andrew Jackson!

The story gets even more tragic, however. When Jackson ran for president in 1828, incumbent John Quincy Adams and his supporters were relentless in using the story of his "adulterous" marriage to smear Jackson's otherwise popular image. Jackson, who was strong and a fighter, was able to weather the attacks and persevere in his drive to win the presidency. Rachel, on the other hand, did not fare so well. The scandalous charges being made against her honor were more than she could handle—first she slipped into a deep depression. Then, following the election, she had a massive heart attack and died before she even had a chance to see her husband take office.

She was buried three days before Christmas in the gown she had planned to wear to the Inaugural Ball.

PRESIDENT: **Martin Van Buren**

THE SCOOP: None, although his VP, Richard Johnson, was publicly known to be the father of two illegitimate children. Perhaps Johnson would have married Julia Chinn, his mistress and the mother of his children, if he could have—but the law forbade it since she was black and he was her master.

Sex!

PRESIDENTS: **William Henry Harrison, John Tyler, James Polk, Zachary Taylor, Millard Fillmore, Franklin Pierce**

THE SCOOP: Not a cheater in the bunch.

PRESIDENT: **James Buchanan**
CHEATED ON WHOM: **???**
CHEATED WITH WHOM: **???**

THE SCOOP: Why did James Buchanan's fiancée commit suicide? [Hint: You can find the answer on page 71.]

a. Because she suspected Buchanan had a girlfriend.
b. Because she suspected Buchanan had a boyfriend.
c. None of the above.

PRESIDENT: **Abraham Lincoln**

THE SCOOP: **He never cheated on his wife. He left her standing at the altar instead**
It's true. It was New Year's Day 1841. Mary Todd was at the appointed place at the appointed time, surrounded by friends, a preacher, and a lot of flowers . . . but Abe never showed. They finally did marry two years later—this time with two hours' notice.

PRESIDENT: **Andrew Johnson**

THE SCOOP: Nope.

PRESIDENT: **Rutherford B. Hayes**

THE SCOOP: Nothing here.

PRESIDENT: **Ulysses S. Grant**

THE SCOOP: Nope.

PRESIDENT: **James Garfield**
CHEATED ON WHOM: **Lucretia Garfield**
CHEATED WITH WHOM: **Mrs. Calhoun**

THE SCOOP: The marriage of James and Lucretia Garfield was a rocky one. Once, while a Civil War general all alone in a strange town, he met a woman. He liked her; she liked him. They had an affair.

Not much is known about Garfield and Mrs. Calhoun because once Mrs. Garfield found out about the affair she sent her husband back for one last visit with his New York mistress. (But he didn't make the trip to make love. Instead, he went back to collect all the love letters he had sent so they wouldn't surface later and ruin his political career.)

Sex!

PRESIDENT: **Chester A. Arthur**

THE SCOOP: Nope.

PRESIDENT: **Grover Cleveland**

THE SCOOP: See *Grover Cleveland's Love-Child-of-the-Month Club* on page 25.

PRESIDENT: **William H. Taft**

THE SCOOP: Nah.

> "You can't cast a man as a Romeo who looks
> and acts so much like an apothecary's clerk."
> —TEDDY ROOSEVELT, OF HIS OPPONENT WOODROW WILSON

PRESIDENT: Woodrow Wilson

CHEATED ON WHOM: His first wife, Ellen

CHEATED WITH WHOM: Mary Peck

THE SCOOP: **The Many Loves of the Apothecary, Part One**

Wilson and Mrs. Peck met in Bermuda. He needed a rest, his doctor said. But his salary as the president of Princeton University didn't allow him the luxury of taking his wife along.

Mrs. Peck was separated from her wealthy husband and living the high life in Bermuda, hanging out with the governor and Mark Twain and all sorts of other fascinating people.

Wilson's—and Mrs. Peck's—first visit to Bermuda was in 1907. He returned in 1908 and 1910, all the while carrying on an active correspondence with Mrs. Peck in the time in between.

Wilson's relationship with Mrs. Peck made for good newspaper copy when Wilson became a contender for the presidency and when he ran for reelection. When *Mr. Peck* filed for divorce it was rumored that Wilson was to be named in the suit. It was also rumored that Wilson's letters to Mrs. Peck would be used as evidence. But none of that came to pass.

In reality Wilson had nothing to hide. He had already told his wife about his platonic but treasured friendship with Mrs. Peck, and in an effort to put an end to the rumors once he won the Democratic Party's nomination for the presidency, he took his entire family to Bermuda to meet her.

Later, Mrs. Peck visited the Wilsons at the White House and even spent a day on a shopping spree with Mrs. Wilson.

The Many Loves of the Apothecary, Part Two

While Wilson was president, his wife died of Bright's disease—and it didn't take long for rumors to surface that romantically linking Wilson and Mrs. Peck again.

In reality, however, those rumors couldn't have been farther from the truth. It was true that Wilson began seeing another woman a year after his wife died and that he did propose to her just two months after they met—but that woman was a widow named Edith Galt, not Mrs. Peck.

Call It a Freudian Slip

After Wilson and Mrs. Galt announced their engagement the *Washington Post* ran an exclusive front-page story about the couple's first day in public. While the writer of the story reported that the president spent the day "entertaining" his new fiancée, no one at the paper caught the typo that announced in large type: ". . . the President spent the afternoon entering his new fiancée."

WHITE HOUSE: CONFIDENTIAL

PRESIDENT: Warren G. Harding
CHEATED ON WHOM: His wife, Florence
CHEATED WITH WHOM: Nan Britton and Carrie Phillips

THE SCOOP: See *Mistresses: The Warren G. Harding Way* on page 77.

PRESIDENT: Calvin Coolidge

THE SCOOP: Old Silent Cal? Nothing to tell.

PRESIDENT: Herbert Hoover

THE SCOOP: Are you kidding? Hoover was an engineer.

PRESIDENT: Franklin Delano Roosevelt
CHEATED ON WHOM: His wife, Eleanor
CHEATED WITH WHOM: Lucy Mercer and Missy LeHand

THE SCOOP: Without presidents like FDR, there wouldn't be books like this one. Or have you already forgotten the first story in this book?

PRESIDENT: Harry S Truman

THE SCOOP: Nope.

PRESIDENT: Dwight D. Eisenhower
CHEATED ON WHOM: His wife, Mamie
CHEATED WITH WHOM: Kay Summersby

THE SCOOP: **Ike almost had an affair. . . .**
While a general during World War Two, Ike had a driver in London who was a very attractive model and actress named Kay Summersby. Later, when he took full command of the European Theatre of Operation, he requested that she be assigned to him as his full-time driver.

According to one account, after the war Eisenhower had written to his superior requesting reassignment in the United States so he could divorce his wife and marry Kay. Kay later wrote a tell-all about her affair with Ike called *Past Forgetting: My Love Affair with Dwight D. Eisenhower.* The irony is, there wasn't much to tell, for according to Summersby, Ike was impotent.

> "This administration's going to do for sex
> what the last one did for golf."
> —JFK SPEECHWRITER THEODORE SORENSEN

PRESIDENT: John F. Kennedy

CHEATED ON WHOM: His wife, Jackie

CHEATED WITH WHOM: Perhaps it would be easier to list the names of the few glamorous and beautiful women of the time he didn't sleep with.

THE SCOOP: On second thought, that wouldn't be half as much fun as listing the names of some he allegedly did sleep with: Marilyn Monroe, Jayne Mansfield, Audrey Hepburn, Angie Dickinson, stripper Blaze Starr, and gangster moll Judith Campbell Exner. And let's not forget Marlene Dietrich, who claimed to have slept with JFK and JFK's brother Joe Jr., and JFK's father, Joe Sr. This short list does not include the names of hundreds (yes, hundreds) of other women JFK is said to have slept with. Of course, supplying names of more than a handful of his lovers would be impossible since it is doubtful even Kennedy knew them all by name.

Or, to quote the book *Presidential Sex* by Wesley O. Hagood:

Jack had numerous sexual encounters with many women. Some were well-known movie stars and burlesque queens. Others were high-class call girls and common prostitutes. His sexual partners also included White House Staffers, secretaries, stewardesses, socialites, campaign workers, and acquaintances of his trusted male friends. Hundreds of others will probably never come to light.

For fun, let's focus on two of his affairs:

Jack Kennedy and Marilyn Monroe

Their regular meeting places included his sister Patricia's home in Santa Monica (she was married to actor Peter Lawford) and the Beverly Hilton Hotel. And they even got together for dalliances at the White House when Jackie was away and when he was aboard *Air Force One*. In 1961 JFK attended a Christmas party at the Lawford home without Jackie and ended up spending several hours alone with Monroe. The entire intimate event, in which the two soaked together in a tub, showered each other with champagne, and more, was caught on tape by a private investigator hired by Jimmy Hoffa, the head of the Teamsters' Union.

The affair led Marilyn to believe the president was going to leave Jackie and marry her . . . which obviously spelled trouble for JFK. Younger brother Bobby was dispatched to delicately make it clear to Marilyn she would never be the First Lady. Once Bobby helped her see the light, he had a passionate affair with her himself. And when she began to have the same delusions about him, he dumped her just as JFK had done.

But Marilyn was stubborn, delusional, and in love. And she had the ear of anyone in the press she wanted—in other words, she represented real danger to the president and the whole of the Kennedy clan. On August 4, 1962, Bobby made a special trip to Los Angeles to convince her their relationship was over. Hours later, she killed herself.

JFK and Judith Campbell Exner

She was Sam Giancana's mistress, and he was a huge mob boss. Of course, when the year is 1960 and you are running for president and you want your friends to introduce you to women who are accessible, willing, and stunningly beautiful, you either need friends in Hollywood (see Jack Kennedy and Marilyn Monroe above) or friends who hang out with gangsters—since gangsters always have beautiful girlfriends hanging around.

Or you could make the process a whole lot easier by having friends who were comfortable in both the world of Hollywood and the world of underground crime.

Those who can read between the lines can see the name Frank Sinatra printed there, for he's the one who introduced the president to Sam Giancana's moll.

What did JFK see in Campbell? Well, she was a stunner, first of all. And second, she had once been Sinatra's mistress, so that added to the appeal. Then, of course, there was the fact that brother Ted had made a pass at her earlier in the evening and had been rebuffed by her—and no Kennedy boy could pass up the chance to best one of his brothers.

The two lovers met all over the country: at the Kennedy home in Georgetown, at a friend's home in Palm Beach, and at the Hilton Hotel in Los Angeles where the Democratic Convention was being held. Once Kennedy was president, the two even met at the White House, and the president once invited Campbell to join him on *Air Force One*.

> ## "Yes! I remember her. She was great!"
> —JFK, WHEN AIDES SHOWED HIM A SNAPSHOT OF HIM AND AN UNNAMED WOMAN SUNBATHING IN THE NUDE

"We Learned It All from Dad!"

In spite of the fact that JFK's father had married into one of the most prominent families in Boston and then fathered nine children (Joe Jr., JFK, Rosemary, Kathleen, Eunice, Patricia, Bobby, Jean, and Teddy), he made a career of womanizing. In the early days of his marriage he had late-night affairs aplenty with hat-check girls and women of unsavory reputation. Later, as a Hollywood mogul, his tastes became more refined; he counted among his mistresses stars like Gloria Swanson and a host of others. But you didn't have to be a Hollywood starlet to be one of Joe Sr.'s girls.

Nellie Bly, in her book *The Kennedy Men,* tells this story:

Jack [JFK] liked to tell friends about the time one of his sisters' friends woke in the middle of the night at Hyannis and saw the Ambassador [JFK's father] standing next to her bed, beginning to take his robe off as he whispered, "This is going to be something you'll always remember." Jack had watched the scene through a keyhole and took to warning female guests: "Be sure to lock the bedroom door. The Ambassador has a tendency to prowl late at night."

"Move over. This is your president."

—LBJ, TO A FEMALE STAFFER AFTER APPEARING AT THE FOOT OF HER BED IN THE MIDDLE OF THE NIGHT

PRESIDENT: Lyndon Baines Johnson

CHEATED ON WHOM: His wife, Lady Bird Johnson

CHEATED WITH WHOM: Alice Glass, Madeline Brown, and many others if you believed LBJ

THE SCOOP: LBJ was a known womanizer—and he was known as such because he loved bragging about his exploits. Perhaps the story that best illustrates his attitude toward extramarital affairs occurred while one of his female staffers was with him on a working trip to the Johnson ranch in Texas. In the middle of the night, the staffer reported, a figure in a white sleeping shirt appeared at the foot of her bed. "Move over!" the figure ordered. "This is your president."

Madeline Brown, on the other hand, was more than a one-night stand. She claims she was LBJ's mistress and sexual plaything for twenty-one years and the mother of his son. In return for satisfying Johnson sexually, LBJ gave Brown a two-bedroom house, a new car every few years, a maid, and the use of a host of credit cards.

But when it comes to longevity, Alice Glass had Madeline Brown beat. She met LBJ while he was a young congressman. He was no doubt impressed with Alice's stunning good looks and her intellectual charms; she was impressed with LBJ's commitment to the same causes she was—particularly the wars against poverty, racism, and discrimination. They had an affair that lasted almost thirty years—but after all that time she stopped sleeping with him because she strongly disagreeed with his actions and policies in Vietnam.

"Of course, I may go into a strange bedroom every now and then that I don't want you to write about, but otherwise you can write everything."

—LBJ, IN A STATEMENT TO THE PRESS

WHITE HOUSE: CONFIDENTIAL

PRESIDENT: Richard Nixon

CHEATED ON WHOM: His wife, Pat

CHEATED WITH WHOM: Marianna Liu

THE SCOOP: **Sex and Richard Nixon? Get real!**

Or so we would have thought until we read about Marianna Liu, a beautiful Chinese cocktail waitress he met in 1958 while on a trip to Hong Kong as Ike's VP. When Nixon's term as VP ended he returned again to Hong Kong in 1964, 1965, and 1966 to see Marianna. On one memorable night Nixon and his good friend Bebe Rebozo visited Marianna at The Den, the cocktail lounge where she was hostess. Later that night, Marianna and a friend visited Nixon and Rebozo in their hotel suite to share "drinks and fruit."

Nixon's relationship with Marianna was of special interest to investigators in Hong Kong because Marianna was suspected of being a communist spy. The relationship became of greater interest to them after Nixon declared his candidacy for the presidency. After all, if Nixon became president—and he and Marianna were having an affair and she was a communist spy—any tape recordings and photos or other materials she had could be used to blackmail him and the American government and the American people.

Marianna finally emigrated to the U.S. in 1969, choosing the town of Whittier, California, to settle in. Whittier just happened to be Nixon's hometown. After she became a permanent resident of the United States, she visited Nixon twice at the White House. Their relationship ended shortly afterward, however, because, as one source says, Pat Nixon was "on to it."

PRESIDENT: Gerald Ford

THE SCOOP: **Surrounded by good wine and good food and with a beautiful young aide, the vice president was found barefoot and dead. . . .** Gerald Ford may have kept his nose clean, but his VP, Nelson Rockefeller, died of a heart attack one night at the age of seventy while "editing an art book" with an attractive twenty-five-year-old aide. When paramedics arrived, they found wine and food on the table but no art and no manuscript. Meanwhile, Rockefeller was lying on the floor sans shoes or socks while the aide, Megan Marshak, was dressed in a long black evening gown.

> ## "I hope you made my grandfather happy."
>
> —ROCKEFELLER'S EIGHTEEN-YEAR-OLD GRANDSON, STEVEN, WHEN ASKED WHAT HE WOULD SAY TO MARSHAK IF HE HAD A CHANCE TO MEET HER

PRESIDENT: Jimmy Carter

CHEATED ON WHOM: His wife, Rosalynn (sort of)

CHEATED WITH WHOM: He didn't really say.

THE SCOOP: While running for president in 1976, Jimmy Carter ended an interview with *Playboy* magazine with a final thought intended to explain his relationship with God. Instead he put his foot in his mouth:

I try not to commit a deliberate sin. I recognize that I'm going to do it anyhow because I'm human and I'm tempted. And Christ set some almost impossible standards for us. Christ said, "I'll tell you that anyone who looks on a woman with lust in his heart has already committed adultery."

I've looked on a lot of women with lust. I've committed adultery in my heart many times.

PRESIDENT: **Ronald Reagan**

THE SCOOP: Nothing to tell. (But there have been some good rumors about Nancy and Frank Sinatra.)

PRESIDENT: **George Bush**
CHEATED ON WHOM: **His wife, Barbara**
CHEATED WITH WHOM: **Allegedly with an aide named Jennifer Fitzgerald and others**

THE SCOOP: When a *CNN* reporter asked George Bush in 1992 about an alleged affair with his longtime aide, Jennifer Fitzgerald, he responded:

I'm not going to take any sleazy questions like that from CNN. I am very disappointed that you would ask such a question of me, and I will not respond to it. I haven't responded in the past, and I think it's an outrage.

Sex!

It was the first time a reporter had ever asked a sitting president if he had ever had an affair.

Granted, CNN reporter Mary Tillotson displayed bad timing with her question . . . for standing right next to the president at the time was Israel's prime minister, Yitzhak Rabin. However, it is also important to note how Bush answered the question.

He didn't.

If you think about it, catching a president at adultery is pretty tricky business. After all, it's all idle speculation unless there's a mistress (or mistresses) who spills her guts or eyewitnesses who spill the beans.

Such is the case of George Bush—there's lots of innuendo from Democrats and various members of the press. But it's all circumstantial:

- In the summer of 1992 the cover of *Spy* magazine was devoted to a story called "1,000 Reasons Not to Vote for George Bush." The first reason the article cited for not voting for Bush? *Because he cheats on his wife.*

  The story by Joe Conason, who is the executive editor of the *New York Observer,* covered the Jennifer Fitzgerald story in detail, and alludes to as many as five other mistresses as well. And even though it is still all circumstantial, Conason sums things up well when he says:

If all the proof needed were what people who know him well say in private or off the record about George Bush, he would have been pilloried as a philanderer years ago.

- In 1986 a *CNN* reporter interviewed Louis Fields, a U.S. ambassador to the Geneva nuclear disarmament talks. Louis confessed that he had once arranged for then Vice President Bush and his aide Jennifer Fitzgerald to "use" a guest house in 1984. "It became very clear to me that the vice president and Ms. Fitzgerald were romantically involved. It made me very uncomfortable." Unfortunately, Fields died in 1988, so he's not available for further comment.

- Kitty Kelley, in her biography of Nancy Reagan, tells the story of a group of people having dinner in Washington, D.C.:

  "Suddenly, there was a great commotion," recalled one of the five dinner guests, "as the security men accompanying the secretary of state [Alexander Haig] and the attorney general [William French Smith] converged on our table. They started jabbering into their walkie-talkies, and then whispered to Haig and Smith, who both jumped up and left the restaurant. The two men returned about forty-five minutes later, laughing their heads off. They said they had to bail out George Bush, who'd been in a traffic accident with his girlfriend. Bush had not wanted the incident to appear on the D.C. police blotter, so he had his security men contact Haig and Smith. They took care of things for him, and then came back to dinner."

Even though Kelley got this story firsthand from people who were there at the dinner, it's still all just circumstantial evidence.

PRESIDENT: Bill Clinton

CHEATED ON WHOM: His wife, Hillary Rodham Clinton

CHEATED WITH WHOM: No mystery here. Gennifer Flowers told PENTHOUSE magazine all about her twelve-year affair with Clinton while he served as governor of Arkansas. The names of a handful of other women have also been linked to Clinton since he married Hillary Rodham Clinton in 1975 and was first elected governor in 1979. In many cases the damning evidence of these affairs comes from the state troopers who were hired to protect Clinton while he was governor. But nothing has been proven . . . yet.

THE SCOOP: Uh, uh. we're not touching this until our friends have put as much money into our defense fund as Clinton's friends have put into his. If you'd like to know more about Bill's alleged extramarital affairs, we recommend you read today's—or any day's—paper.

NEWSFLASH!: As we send this book to press, the Monica Lewinsky story is breaking on the wire. As all of America—and the world—wonders if he did or didn't, the problem is obvious. When you're a suspected philanderer, you become an easy mark, even if the truth is that you didn't. Stay tuned for details.

PRESIDENTIAL "SCORECARD"

WHAT IF PRESIDENTS WERE BALLPLAYERS and it was Dan Rather's job to fill time every night with a lot of meaningless statistics? Suddenly the evening news makes a lot of sense.

*A Chronological Chart of "Sinners"**

Years	President(s)	Length of Term	Sinner	Non-Sinner
1789–1797	George Washington	8 years	✔	
1797–1801	John Adams	4 years		✔
1801–1809	Thomas Jefferson	8 years	✔	
1809–1817	James Madison	8 years		✔
1817–1825	James Monroe	8 years		✔
1825–1829	John Quincy Adams	4 years		✔
1829–1837	Andrew Jackson	8 years		✔
1837–1841	Martin Van Buren	4 years		✔
1841–1841	William Henry Harrison	1 month		✔

* *As defined by Jimmy Carter.*

Sex!

Years	President(s)	Length of Term	Sinner	Non-Sinner
1841-1845	John Tyler	4 years		✔
1845-1849	James Polk	4 years		✔
1849-1850	Zachary Taylor	16 months		✔
1850-1853	Millard Fillmore	3 years		✔
1853-1857	Franklin Pierce	4 years		✔
1857-1861	James Buchanan	4 years	✔	
1861-1865	Abraham Lincoln	4 years		✔
1865-1869	Andrew Johnson	4 years		✔
1869-1877	Ulysses S. Grant	8 years		✔
1877-1881	Rutherford B. Hayes	4 years		✔
1881-1881	James Garfield	2.5 months	✔	
1881-1885	Chester Alan Arthur	4 years		✔
1885-1889	Grover Cleveland	4 years	✔	
1889-1893	Benjamin Harrison	4 years		✔
1893-1897	Grover Cleveland	4 years	✔	
1897-1901	William McKinley	4 years		✔

Years	President(s)	Length of Term	Sinner	Non-Sinner
1901-1909	Theodore Roosevelt	8 years		✔
1909-1913	William Howard Taft	4 years		✔
1913-1921	Woodrow Wilson	8 years		✔
1921-1923	Warren G. Harding	2 years	✔	
1923-1929	Calvin Coolidge	6 years		✔
1929-1933	Herbert Hoover	4 years		✔
1933-1945	Franklin D. Roosevelt	12 years	✔	
1945-1953	Harry Truman	8 years		✔
1953-1961	Dwight D. Eisenhower	8 years	✔	
1961-1963	John F. Kennedy	2 years	✔	
1963-1969	Lyndon B. Johnson	6 years	✔	
1969-1974	Richard Nixon	5 years	✔	
1974-1977	Gerald Ford	3 years		✔
1977-1981	Jimmy Carter*	4 years	✔	
1981-1989	Ronald Reagan	8 years		✔

* By his definition, not ours.

Years	President(s)	Length of Term	Sinner	Non-Sinner
1989-1993	George Bush	4 years	✔	
1993-	Bill Clinton	5+ years	✔	

How to Calculate Which Party Has Had More "Sinners"* in the White House

- *T*here have been forty-one presidents including Bill Clinton.
- Although Grover Cleveland served two nonconsecutive terms as our twenty-second and twenty-fourth president, he only counts once in the head count above.
- It wasn't until the election of 1852, when Franklin Pierce was elected, that the two-party system as we know it came into existence. For that reason the following statistics apply only to the years 1852 to 1996. The one exception was the election of Andrew Johnson to vice president in 1864; he was a Democrat nominated for VP by the Republicans and elected with Lincoln on the National Union ticket.
- Since the election of 1852 twenty-eight men have served as president—eleven as Democrats and seventeen as Republicans.
- Since the election of 1852 a Republican president has been in the White House for eighty years and a Democrat for sixty-six years.

As defined by Jimmy Carter.

"Sinners"* by Party

Democrats	Republicans	Third Party
1. James Buchanan	1. James Garfield	1. George Washington (Federalist)
2. Grover Cleveland	2. Warren G. Harding	2. Thomas Jefferson (Democrat-Republican)
3. Franklin D. Roosevelt	3. Dwight D. Eisenhower	
4. John F. Kennedy	4. Richard Nixon	
5. Lyndon B. Johnson	5. George Bush	
6. Jimmy Carter**		
7. Bill Clinton		

* As defined by Jimmy Carter.

** Again, by his definition, not ours.

PRESIDENTIAL MISTRESS*/GIRLFRIEND** NAMING CHART

Just a little advice for parents: If you want your daughter to grow up to be the mistress or girlfriend of the president, just give her a name that is some variation of Mary. Second runner-up: Jennifer (if you want your daughter to grow to have an affair with a Republican) or Gennifer (if you want to see her playing around with a Democrat).

President	Alleged Mistress	Alleged Girlfriend	Other
George Washington		Sally Fairfax (married)	
Thomas Jefferson		Betsey Walker (married) **Maria** Cosway (married) Sally Hemings (underage slave)	
James Buchanan			William D. King
James Garfield	Mrs. Calhoun		
Grover Cleveland		**Maria** Halpin (may have conceived an illegitimate child together)	
Warren G. Harding	Nan Britton Carrie Philips		
FDR	Lucy Mercer **Mar**guerite (Missy) LeHand		

WHITE HOUSE: CONFIDENTIAL

President	Alleged Mistress	Alleged Girlfriend	Other
Dwight D. Eisenhower	Kay Summersby		
John F. Kennedy	**Mari**lyn Monroe Marlene Dietrich Jayne Mansfield Angie Dickinson Blaze Starr Judith Campbell Exner, etc.		
LBJ	Alice Glass Madeline Brown		
Richard Nixon	**Maria**nna Liu		
George Bush	**Jennifer** Fitzgerald		
Bill Clinton	**Gennifer** Flowers		

* A presidential mistress is defined as a woman who has been involved with a married president.

** A presidential girlfriend is defined as a woman who has been involved with a bachelor president under immoral circumstances.

3

SCANDAL!

DUH!"

That's the sound of a really good presidential scandal once it makes the papers and reaches your average guy or gal on the street. It's usually followed up with "How could this guy, the president, be so stupid?" or "How could he be so stupid that he actually got caught?"

The measure of a good scandal is the look on the president's face at the moment he gets nailed. Then comes the denial, the st-st-stuttering attempt to explain, or the dance to place blame on the back of someone else. And that's when the show starts to get good.

Let's define a good scandal, shall we? Essentially, there are two types:

1. The first begins with an event or set of circumstances that are not very important, yet are easily described in a few words or sentences and are easily blown out of proportion by the press. From a consumer's point of view, this type of scandal is one that leaves us all with an insatiable desire to know more. And every time another fact or angle is added to the story, it sounds even more ludicrous or surreal or dumb than it did before, driving us to want to know even *more*.

2. The second type of scandal is more serious. It usually involves a serious breech of security or confidence or trust, yet is equally as dumb.

Bill Clinton's two-hundred-dollar haircut on a runway at LAX was a good scandal of the former variety. Ronald Reagan's Iran-Contra affair is a fine example of the latter. Whenever either story is told, it always ends with those same two questions: "How could this guy, the president, be so stupid?" or "How could he be so stupid that he actually got caught?"

ALEXANDER HAMILTON'S BLACKMAILING MISTRESS

It just goes to show you that you don't have to be president to create a presidential-sized scandal.

Just ask Alexander Hamilton, a guy who was secretary of the treasury and might have become president one day if Vice President Aaron Burr hadn't killed him first.

When it came to politics, Hamilton may have been smart. But as the following story shows, when it came to having an affair he was a real sucker.

In a Nutshell, Hamilton Was Set Up

It was a beautiful plan, one created by a sultry and seductive woman named Maria Reynolds (yet another of our fearless leaders finds himself compromising his virtue with yet another woman named Maria) and her husband, James, who was a con man. It worked like this:

- First, Maria paid a visit to Hamilton at his office and told him a long and tragic tale of being deserted by her husband.
- Next, she lured him back to her house for a tryst—for which Hamilton paid her handsomely. The payment, no doubt, was Hamilton's way of helping Maria deal with the financial aspect of her desertion plight.
- Now the plot thickened . . . for in walked Maria's husband.

Hamilton Has a Problem

*F*rom a blackmailer's perspective, it doesn't get any better than this—Hamilton had a wife, a reputation, and a future in politics to protect. And here is where James and Maria Reynolds proved they were not your common lowlife blackmailers wanting to make a quick buck and run. No, what they had in mind for Hamilton was a long-term financial plan.

James Reynolds's initial reaction to finding his wife with another man was one of shock and horror—his wife was taken from him! His home was broken! His heart would never heal! (Of course, Reynolds was only acting; this was all part of a larger plan.)

On second thought, James Reynolds said to Alexander Hamilton, maybe this isn't such a bad thing after all. You seem to like Maria, she seems to like you, and she seems to be in a better mood after she has seen you. If you'll just pay me a thousand dollars, you can sleep with my wife any time you like, and no one has to be any wiser.

The attraction was mutual—James and Maria liked Hamilton's money, and Hamilton was infatuated with Maria. The affair continued for almost a year.

The World According to James Reynolds:

"You took advantage of a poor Broken harted woman. . . . You have acted the part of the most Cruelest man in existence. . . . Now Sire you have bin the Cause of Cooling [of] her affections for me."

—James Reynolds, before Hamilton paid him off

★ ★ ★

"I find when ever you have been with her, she is Cheerful and kind, but when you have not in some time she is Quite the Reverse."

—Reynolds, after Hamilton paid him off

Scandal!

After Hamilton paid him the first thousand dollars James Reynolds of course continued to ask for more. Hamilton paid it, at times even borrowing money from friends to keep James and Maria happy.

And Baby Makes Four

This cash-for-sex relationship with James and Maria Reynolds continued for almost a year until Maria got pregnant and threatened to kill herself. To Hamilton, this looked like a smart time to bow out. However, James Reynolds saw things differently: He decided it was the perfect time to ask for more than money—this time he tried to blackmail Hamilton into giving him a nice, cushy government job.

This is where Hamilton drew the line. His personal life was his own to make a mess of, he reasoned, but to his credit, he was completely unwilling to compromise his position or the public trust.

James, on the other hand, figured that if he couldn't get a government appointment or any more money out of Hamilton, then he could certainly earn some cash by taking the entire story to Hamilton's political enemies in Congress.

Hamilton Spills His Guts

On December 15, 1792, Democrat Alexander Hamilton responded to a knock at his door and opened it to discover three Republican congressmen—James Monroe, Frederick Muhlenburg, and Abraham Venable—standing on his doorstep and ready to string him up.

The Reynolds Wrap-Up

★ ★ ★

Here's how the saga of James and Maria Reynolds ended:

- Maria eventually divorced James and married another con man.
- Maria's attorney for her divorce was none other than Aaron Burr.
- Maria was not only an adulteress; she was also a bigamist. It seems she got married again thirty minutes before Burr got her divorce finalized.

James Reynolds, it seems, not only told these three congressmen about Hamilton's affair, but he also led them to believe Hamilton had used government funds to pay him off.

As Hamilton saw it, if he was going to avoid hanging right there or public humiliation later, he had to convince the three guys in his living room that, while on a personal level his actions were immoral, he hadn't done anything to compromise his position as secretary of the treasury. And the only way Hamilton could see to convince these guys, his political enemies, was to tell them every last detail of the affair and to document his story with a well-laid paper trail. Hamilton's story was so convincing and so well documented—he had signed receipts for money borrowed from friends, signed receipts he had given to James, and love letters he had received from Maria—that the three congressmen could in no way doubt his story.

The three congressmen heard him out.

As much as they would have liked to use the story to destroy him, they were concerned that a scandal of this nature, involving such a high-ranking member of the government when the Union was so young, could destroy the people's confidence in their leaders and their nation—and so all three agreed to carry Hamilton's story to the grave.

Hamilton's story remained secret for six years until a written transcript of his confession was leaked to the press and published. Hamilton quickly retaliated with his own published response that, interestingly, went on to become a bestseller.

Everything I know about [bad] karma I learned from Vice President Aaron Burr.

- He was the first presidential candidate to lose the presidency by a vote of the House of Representatives.
- Next he was passed over by his own party for reelection as vice president.
- Finally, that lug Alexander Hamilton called him "despicable" and "dangerous" and, well, what else could Burr do but challenge him to a duel and kill him?
- But what goes around comes around: Aaron Burr died in 1836 at the age of eighty a forgotten man without a cent to his name in a hotel on Staten Island in New York City.

Was James Buchanan
America's first gay president?

★ ★ ★

Was William Rufus DeVane King
America's first gay vice president?

★ ★ ★

Were the president and the
vice president having an affair?

WAS HE OR WASN'T HE?

*T*his is a story of sexual intrigue that involves a president, a vice president, a fiancée, and a closet.

Although they were president and vice president during different administrations, James Buchanan and William Rufus De Vane King may have been the first gay men to occupy the executive offices of the United States of America. They met as members of Congress. King was elected to the Senate from the state of Alabama at the age of thirty-three in 1819. Buchanan was elected to the Senate from the state of Pennsylvania at the age of forty-three in 1834.

From the moment they met, they were inseparable. For years, they were known as "Miss Nancy and Aunt Fancy" or "Mr. Buchanan and his wife" and King was often referred to as "Mrs. B." or "Buchanan's better half."

Did Buchanan's Fiancée Kill Herself When He Told Her the News?

*A*t the age of twenty-eight Buchanan was engaged to Anne Coleman, who died suddenly of mysterious causes. The truth of her death remains unknown, but many historians believe she committed suicide.

This much is known: Buchanan never became involved with another woman for the rest of his life.

Or . . . Was James Buchanan "Outed"?

A day after Anne's death, Buchanan sent a letter to her father:

My Dear Sir:

You have lost a child, a dear, dear child. I have lost the only earthly object of my affections, without whom life now presents to me a dreary blank. My prospects are all cut off, and I feel that my happiness will be buried with her in the grave. It is now no time for explanation, but the time will come when you will discover that she, as well as I, have been much abused. God forgive the authors of it. My feelings of resentment against them, whoever they may be, are buried in the dust. I have now one request to make, and, for the love of God and of your dear departed daughter whom I loved infinitely more than any other human being could love, deny me not. Afford me the melancholy pleasure of seeing her body before its internment. I would not for the world be denied this request.

I might make another, but from the misrepresentations which must have been made to you, I am almost afraid. I would like to follow her remains to the grave as a mourner. I would like to convince the world, and I hope yet to convince you, that she was infinitely dearer to me than life. I may sustain the shock of her death, but I feel that happiness has fled from me forever. The prayer which I make to God without ceasing is, that I yet may be able to show my veneration for the memory of my dear departed saint, by my respect and attachment for her surviving friends.

May Heaven bless you, and enable you to bear the shock with the fortitude of a Christian. I am, forever, your sincere and grateful friend,

James Buchanan

Anne Coleman's father returned the letter unopened.

Will the "Real" Story Behind Anne Coleman's Death Ever Be Known?

At one point in his seventies, James Buchanan seemed ready to reveal the details of his relationship with her and the cause of her death. He told a friend he had deposited documents at a bank in New York that would explain his relationship with Miss Coleman.

Unfortunately, after Buchanan died his executors found a handwritten note with the documents instructing them to destroy the papers without reading them . . . and they followed his instructions to the letter.

Or so they said.

But if they didn't do as Buchanan asked and they did read the documents before they destroyed them, they sure kept their mouths shut tight about what they knew. Nothing new about Buchanan's love life, other than rumors and speculation and innuendo, has ever been revealed.

THE STRANGE CASE OF THE ALCOHOLIC AND THE DYING MAN

A Further Scandal Involving William Rufus Devane King

While running as Franklin Pierce's vice-presidential candidate, King didn't do a single day of campaigning.

Why? Because he was holed up in Havana dying of tuberculosis.

President-to-be Franklin Pierce wasn't in much better shape . . . he was such a heavy drinker that Republicans would taunt him by calling him "a hero . . . of many a well-fought bottle."

While Pierce was able to control his drinking well enough to make it through four years in the White House, King didn't have the same luck. He was so sick that he didn't even make it back to Washington for his inauguration. Instead, by a special act of Congress, he was allowed to be sworn into office in Cuba—in fact, he's the only executive officer of the United States that has ever been sworn in on foreign soil. King died six weeks after taking office and didn't spend a single day of his vice-presidential term in the capital city.

WARREN G. HARDING GETS EXISTENTIAL

Duh-mb!

When it became apparent that the charming, handsome Ohio newspaperman Warren Harding was to be a strong contender for the Republican presidential nomination in 1920, a group of party heavies whisked him into a "smoke-filled" hotel room to grill him about his past and any skeletons he might have to hide. When asked directly, Harding responded by dismissing himself from the room for a break. He was gone for close to ten minutes and when he returned he told the waiting Republicans there wasn't anything he was hiding that would surface later and harm his reputation.

Perhaps Harding misunderstood the question. While the party bosses wanted to know if he had any skeletons to hide, Harding must have thought they just wanted to make sure all his skeletons were well hidden.

"Where'd you go, Warren G. Harding?"

Of course, you might choose to believe he was so excited at the prospect of being nominated president that he had to make a quick trip to the bathroom. Most historians, however, figure he slipped out to make a few phone calls. To his mistress. Or mistresses. To beg for their silence.

It worked too. Until Harding dropped dead.

Mistresses: The Warren G. Harding Way

How to Find 'Em

Option #1: If you've got friends and they've got wives, why bother looking anywhere else?

Carrie Phillips was the wive of Harding's good friend Jim Phillips. The Harding-Phillips affair lasted for fifteen years.

Option #2: Let her come to you.

Harding and Nan Britton first met when she was a young teen. He owned the *Marion Star* and she had a secret schoolgirl crush on him and wrote short bits of news for his paper about the activities and students at her school.

Seven years later, when she was twenty-one and living in New York and he was a fifty-one-year-old senator, she contacted him and asked if he could help her get a job.

He could and he did. He took her to a hotel, rented the bridal suite, and offered her a job as his mistress.

Ironically, Nan Britton was a virgin at the time—but that didn't last long. Soon she and the senator were meeting at various hotels and eventually in his Senate offices. After he was elected president they met regularly in a White House closet and in the homes of various Harding friends.

"Whatcha got to hide, Warren G. Harding?"

Plenty:

- A mistress named Carrie Phillips
- Another mistress named Nan Britton
- An illegitimate daughter named Elizabeth Ann Britton

How to Hide 'Em

Option #1: Send her away . . . for life, if you can.

Imagine you're the head of the Republican National Committee and you discover your presidential candidate lied to you about mistresses in that smoke-filled room. Quick! What do you do? How do you keep the press (and the American public) from finding out?

One way: Send her far away to a place where the press will never find her. And send her away for life, if you can.

Believe it or not, this worked with Carrie Phillips. When Harding's campaign manager offered her $25,000 on the spot and $2,000 a month (in 1920 dollars!) to take a long vacation until Harding left office, she took him up on the deal and stayed away until after Harding died.

Option #2: Tell her you love her.

Given the amount of attention that Harding heaped upon Nan there was no way she was going to ruin a good thing by squealing to the press.

Harding sent Nan hundreds of long explicit love letters, letters that ran as long as forty pages in length. Ironically, given Harding's background as a newspaperman, he often chose a pencil and little pieces of scrap paper on which to pour out his deep feelings of love and passion.

WHATEVER HAPPENED TO NAN BRITTON?

The one good thing you could say about Harding was that he really knew how to make friends and he knew how to keep them. The fact that he could get both of his mistresses (and a host of others) to remain quiet about his clandestine affairs during the two and a half years of his presidency was nothing short of a miracle.

Once he died, however, all bets were off. Take the case of Nan Britton: Of course, Harding supplied her with money. Of course he told her he loved her. Of course he led her to believe that he would marry her when his wife died. But he died before his wife and set no money aside for Nan or their daughter. So Nan took matters into her own hands.

First, she tried contacting Harding's family, but they shooed her away. So she naturally did what all good Americans do when in similar straits: She wrote a book.

It was called *The President's Daughter* and was published by the Elizabeth Ann Guild. Elizabeth Ann, of course, was the name of Nan's daughter by Harding, and Britton claimed she would use the money from the sale of the book to help other unwed mothers and illegitimate children.

She must have been able to give others a lot more help than Harding ever gave to her—the book was a runaway bestseller and was made into the movie *Children of No Importance* in 1928.

An Illegitimate Father?

★ ★ ★

Although Elizabeth Ann looked a lot like him, Harding had absolutely no desire to see her. In fact, Nan Britton reported in her book that she could barely get Harding to even look at a photo of her.

Elizabeth Ann was Harding's only child.

POSTSCRIPT TO THE WARREN HARDING STORY

Among historians, it is almost universally accepted that Harding was one of the worst presidents in history.

From the moment he lied about his past in that hotel room, the tone was set for a presidency beset with more lies, corruption, favoritism, and general ineptitude.

The truth about the corruption and favoritism of his administration began to seep out while he was still in office. Financial scandals were uncovered and members of his cabinet resigned and even committed suicide. But the real truth about Harding's presidency wasn't exposed until after he died.

THE PEGGY EATON AFFAIR

Neither of your authors has ever been president, nor do they ever intend to be. But they do have one piece of wisdom to share with you should you ever wind up with the job: Don't ever let your domestic or foreign policy be determined by friends and their domestic problems, as President Andrew Jackson once did.

It all started with President Jackson's friend Senator John Eaton of Tennessee. Senator Eaton had a friend named Peggy Timberlake. Peggy Timberlake had a husband named Captain Timberlake.

Since Captain Timberlake spent a lot of time at sea, Peggy would often get lonely. In fact, let's just say she was what they used to call a woman of "ill repute." The truth is she had a bad reputation with townfolks before Senator Eaton came around—and hanging out with the likes of him didn't help.

Suddenly, one day, Captain Timberlake washed up dead. And President Jackson, with the scandalous affair and death of his own wife, Rachel (see page 35), very much on his mind, urged his friend Senator Eaton to make an honest woman of the now-widowed Mrs. Timberlake. The senator took the president's advice.

So far, so good.

Now, in a totally unrelated move, President Jackson appointed Senator Eaton to the position of secretary of war. While there was no real dispute about Eaton's qualifications to serve in the position, all the society ladies of Washington were appalled. Why? Because if Senator Eaton became secretary of war, it would mean a woman of the former Mrs. Timberlake's virtues, as a result of her new husband's appointment, would necessarily become a member of the Washington wives' inner circle of friends.

Jackson, meanwhile, discounted all the rumors about the new Mrs. Eaton's past and discounted the talk of a Washington Wives' Revolt. Instead he ordered all members of his administration to order all their wives to treat the new Mrs. Eaton with all the dignity and respect her position deserved.

One woman who refused to abide by the president's order was the wife of his own vice president, John Calhoun. President Jackson was so frustrated by Mrs. Calhoun that he called on her at home himself with the intention of delivering the order to her face. However, the will of President Jackson was no match for the will of Floride Calhoun.

Not only did she ignore the president's order to treat Mrs. Eaton with respect, but she gave an order of her own: She told her butler to show the president to the door.

Was Jackson's Reasoning Sound?

★ ★ ★

When Eaton confided in Jackson about Peggy Timberlake's checkered past, the president pointed out that "your marrying her will disprove these charges, and restore Peggy's good name."

It never occurred to President Jackson that his entire cabinet could come unraveled over a scandal involving so small a domestic issue as the reputation of one appointed member's wife. But it did. Given the circumstances that led to the undoing of his own beloved wife's reputation and her death from a heart attack shortly afterward, this entire episode was particularly troubling to President Jackson.

Determined to put things in order and set matters right, President Jackson held a formal dinner for all of his cabinet members and arranged for Peggy Eaton to sit in the seat of honor beside him. The move was intended to send a message to the wives of the other cabinet members. Meanwhile, Mrs. Eaton's choice of attire for the evening didn't do much to help the president's cause; she wore a low-cut dress that covered only one shoulder, which only served to feed the flames of controversy.

President Jackson refused to call a single meeting of his cabinet as long as their wives refused to treat Mrs. Eaton as one of their equals. Therefore, instead of cabinet meetings Jackson held what his enemies called "Kitchen Cabinet" meetings—meetings with trusted friends and advisers who did not hold high public offices but were highly valued and trusted by President Jackson. They were called the Kitchen Cabinet because they usually met in the White House kitchen and snuck in and out through the back door, passing relatively unnoticed.

Peggy Eaton, President-Maker?

The guy who benefited the most from the Eaton affair was President Jackson's secretary of state, Martin Van Buren. He was one of the few members of Jackson's administration who

Jackson may have been the first to have an informal cabinet but he wasn't the last:

Teddy Roosevelt had a Tennis Cabinet, Warren Harding had a Poker Cabinet, and Herbert Hoover had a Medicine Ball Cabinet because he liked to toss one of the heavy balls around while he talked.

could afford to be polite and courteous and attentive toward Mrs. Eaton without risking reprisals at home from his own wife. He was, after all, a widower.

It was Van Buren, in fact, who finally solved the "Petticoat War," as it was called, since the women of Washington were unwilling to let their cause die. His solution: that the president should replace the entire cabinet, letting the pro-Eaton members (like Van Buren and Eaton himself) resign before dismissing the remaining anti-Eaton members. Once he was free of the other members, the president could choose a new Peggy Eaton-friendly cabinet and give his friends Eaton and Van Buren new appointments that were sure to please.

Jackson repaid Van Buren for his brilliant political solution by guaranteeing him his nomination for vice president in the next election.

4

FIGHTS!

SHAKE HANDS AND SAY YOU'RE SORRY."

It's what every dad has said to every son after said son has gotten into a fight. And when you're six or eight or twelve, it actually works.

By the time you get to be president, however, things are all blown out of proportion. It's just not that easy anymore. There's that run for reelection, after all. There's saving face. There's ego and power and political machismo at stake.

So you get into a political skirmish and you kill off a reputation. You get into a battle of ideologies and you kill off a long-standing friendship. Or you go completely off the deep end and kill the man, your opponent, altogether.

Hey, you're president—Leader of the Western world. Killing off your opponent, therefore, is all in a day's work.

GETTING AWAY WITH MURDER! (THE VICE-PRESIDENTIAL WAY)

*L*et's say you're vice president and minding your own business when one day along comes Alexander Hamilton, calling you "despicable" and "dangerous" to your face—what do you do?

If you're Aaron Burr, vice president under Thomas Jefferson, you challenge him to a duel and then swiftly kill him.

Ahh, but *now* what to do?

Let's learn again from Burr. He was charged with murder in New York (where Hamilton actually died) and charged and indicted in New Jersey (where the duel occurred). He might have done what Spiro Agnew did more than a century and a half later, which was to claim that a sitting vice president had the protection of executive privilege and therefore could not be indicted.

"There is nothing I love as much as a good fight."

—FDR

Instead Burr did a far more brilliant thing: He returned to Washington, D.C., and resumed his duties as vice president and president of the Senate as if nothing had happened. Burr knew he was safe since neither New York nor New Jersey had any jurisdiction in Washington, D.C., and thus couldn't extradite him.

Not the End of Burr

Remarkably, Burr was allowed to finish out his term. As the term ended he began to concoct a grand scheme that would allow him not only to get away with the murder of Hamilton but also to involve a group of coconspirators who would help him grab parts of the Louisiana and Orleans Territories. Why? He planned to create and rule an empire that would stretch far into Mexico.

By anyone's definition, what Burr planned was treasonous (not to mention insane), and when Thomas Jefferson got wind of it, he called for Burr's arrest.

By now Burr's life was pretty complicated. First, he was wanted for murder. Second, he was wanted for treason. Third, he found out it was one of his own coconspirators who tipped President Jefferson off to the plan.

So he did the only reasonable thing; he turned himself in. Again he was indicted. This time he stood trial. And miraculously, he was acquitted when Chief Justice John Marshall ruled that one could only be found guilty of an act of treason if the act had been attested to by at least two witnesses.

Again Burr made a wise move: He left the country and didn't return until 1812.

CANDIDATE FOR A CONFLICT-RESOLUTION SEMINAR

James Monroe once got so angry at his secretary of treasury that he chased him out of the White House with a pair of red-hot fire tongs.

On another day, when President Monroe invited the ministers of both Britain and France over to the White House for dinner, things didn't quite work out as planned. In fact, relations got so heated between the two ministers that they got into a fight, and both had their swords drawn before Monroe could break them apart.

"I Shot Him, Sir"

★ ★ ★

Burr wasn't the only one fighting duels. By some accounts, Andrew Jackson was involved in over one hundred—most to defend the honor of his wife, Rachel.

In fact, Jackson was a walking armory: He had a bullet in his chest from an 1806 duel and another in his arm from a barroom fight in 1813.

The barroom shooter was Missouri senator Thomas Hart Benton. When Jackson was elected to the Senate, the two sat side by side and became close friends. Or as Benton said, "General Jackson was a great man. I shot him, sir" and "Yes, I had a fight with Jackson. A fellow was hardly in the fashion who didn't."

RICHARD NIXON: MEANER THAN A JUNKYARD DOG

Well, he may not have had a .32-caliber gun in his pocket or a razor in his shoe, but politically Richard Nixon was every bit as bad as "Bad, Bad Leroy Brown," and he was always getting into fights just like a mean old junkyard dog.

It all started when he was thirty-two and responded to a classified ad in his local newspaper. It was an ad placed by local Republicans; they were holding a talent search for a young veteran who leaned to the right but who had no political experience.

Their goal? To enter the young man into the race for a local seat in the House of Representatives, which had been held by the same Democrat for ten years.

Nixon As a Lightweight

Nixon took to politicking like a piranha. When his wealthy Republican supporters told him to attack, he went straight for his opponent's throat, stretching the truth to make it look like the incumbent—who had recently been named Best Congressman West of the Mississippi by a group of Washington journalists—actually had the support of a communist group.

It was a brilliant strategy on two counts. First, Nixon's opponent was caught off guard and forced to defend himself against mostly baseless charges. Second, even if the incumbent had wanted to retaliate with a negative campaign of his own, Nixon had no political history upon which to draw.

Nixon won 67,874 votes to 49,431, and his political modus operandi was set.

Nixon As a Welterweight

The next time Nixon stepped into the ring, he was a member of the House Un-American Activities Committee and his opponent was Algier Hiss. Nixon rose to national prominence as a result of the Hiss case and was easily reelected to the House of Representatives.

While the Hiss case was for many years a source of great controversy, today historians and political scientists generally agree that Hiss was, in fact, a communist.

Nixon As a Middleweight

It was time for Nixon to run for the Senate. His opponent was incumbent Helen Gahagan Douglas, who had held the seat for four years. It was during this battle that Nixon won the nickname "Tricky Dick." He won the election (and the nickname) by labeling Helen Douglas the "pink lady," then issuing propaganda listing the number of times she and a known communist House member from New York had cast the same votes. While it was true Congresswoman Douglas had voted the same as the communist congressman Marcantonio as many as 354 times, Nixon neglected to mention in his propaganda that he himself had voted the same as Marcantonio 112 times, as had many of his fellow Republicans.

Regardless of the morality of Nixon's charges, they worked, and he won his way into the Senate while also making a name for himself in Washington and nationally.

Years later, when asked about his smear campaign against Congresswoman Douglas, Nixon replied, "I'm sorry about that episode. I was a very young man."

"If I'm a traitor, the United States is in a helluva shape."

—Harry Truman,
upon finding he was the focus of one of
Nixon's communist witch-hunts

Nixon As a Junior Heavyweight

Nixon's next opponent was the press—and he was becoming a smart boxer, learning how to communicate directly with the voter.

When Ike was nominated for president by the Republicans in 1952, Nixon was his first choice for running mate. Nixon, after all, was the perfect foil for Eisenhower's squeaky-clean, paternal image.

Then the trouble began. The *New York Post* ran a story headlined "SECRET NIXON FUND." The story reported that Nixon had a secret eighteen-thousand-dollar slush fund he used to pay for expenses. The story was enough to kill Nixon's career—and given the way he had campaigned in the past, he had a lot of enemies who would have loved to exploit the story. And that was just the Democrats. On the Republican side there were also many who wanted to see Ike drop Nixon from the ticket.

Ike, however, kept a cool head. If Nixon could prove himself innocent and clear his name, Ike said, then he could remain on the ticket. And Ike was more than pleasantly surprised with the result of the flap, for Nixon not only cleared his name but also generated a flood of phone calls and letters to the Republican National Committee demanding he be allowed to remain on the ticket.

Here's how Nixon turned the tide: He used seventy-five thousand dollars of the Republican National Committee's money to speak on national television for thirty minutes about his eighteen-thousand-dollar secret fund. In his speech he exposed the "facts" behind his personal finances: He and his wife, Pat, had a two-year-old Oldsmobile and owned a small amount of equity in their homes in California and Washington, D.C., but had no other real assets like stocks or bonds.

Then Nixon really laid it on strong. "Pat doesn't have a mink coat," he said, "but she does have a respectable Republican cloth coat. And I always tell her she'd look good in anything."

Finally, Nixon's confession:

A man down in Texas heard Pat on the radio mention the fact that our two youngsters would like to have a dog and, believe it or not, the day before we left on this campaign we got a message from Union Station in Washington that they had a package for us. We went down to get it. You know what it was? It was a little cocker spaniel in a crate that had been sent all the way from Texas—black and white, spotted, and our little girl Tricia, the six-year-old, named it Checkers. And you know, the kids, like all kids, loved the dog, and I just want to say this right now, that regardless of what they say about it, we are going to keep it.

Checkers, Anyone?

★ ★ ★

Checkers, by the way, died in 1964 and is buried at the Bide-A-Wee Pet Cemetery on Long Island outside New York City—although there is a movement afoot by the Nixon Library to have him exhumed and reburied next to the president in Yorba Linda, California.

Thus Nixon won the hearts and votes of America . . . and Ike. When Nixon and the general met the next day, Eisenhower greeted Nixon with a handshake, a grin, and the words: "You're my boy."

In spite of his success it should be noted that Nixon at no time during his speech attempted to explain the eighteen-thousand-dollar slush fund.

Nixon Takes His First Loss . . . and His Next . . . and His Next . . .

Following his successful run for the vice presidency as Ike's running mate in 1952 and 1956, Nixon lost his bid for the presidency to Kennedy in 1960. Next he ran for governor of California against incumbent Pat Brown in 1962—and lost. And he lost his battle against the press when he held a press conference on the day after his defeat in the governor's race and announced: "This is my last news conference. . . . You won't have Dick Nixon to kick around any more."

Finally: Nixon as "Heeeeavyweight Chaaaampiiiion of the Woooorld"

Imagine you are visiting a good friend after a long spell has passed. The last time you stopped by, about four years earlier, your friend's eight-year-old son was nothing but trouble; he constantly demanded attention by whatever means it took to get it. He was loud and rude and relentless.

Today, as you stare at the polite, well-spoken twelve-year-old young man before you, you ask yourself, *Is this really the same boy?*

Like a little boy who had finally grown up, Richard Nixon shed his shrill combative shell and became a man who was in control of himself and the world around him. Instead of acting like an attack dog, he began acting like a statesman. Instead of hunting communists, he became a strong proponent of detente with the Soviet Union and a rapprochement with the Communist government of China. This led to the beginning of the Strategic Arms Limitation Talks (SALT) with the Soviets. And in 1972 he traveled to both China and Russia and became the first U.S. president ever to visit either of these countries.

Nixon's first term was not all rosy, however—for the escalation of the Vietnam War cost many lives and caused great strife and havoc at home.

The New Nixon Falls Apart

Call it paranoia or call it fear of failure or give it some other name copped from the annals of pop psychology, but the burglary, the cover-up, and the tapes (missing as well as accounted for)—the string of events most of us call Watergate—were all executed in vain. By most accounts Nixon was already a shoo-in for reelection, even without the "dirty tricks."

PRESIDENT TRUMAN PICKS A FIGHT

Margaret Truman, Harry's daughter, once tried her hand at being a professional singer— but she sure didn't get much praise from the press.

At least one critic, however, found out that criticizing the daughter of the president can be a tricky business. After Paul Hume of the *Washington Post* gave Margaret a negative review he got a letter from her father, the president, warning him that if they ever met he would need "a new nose and plenty of beefsteak."

"HEY, HEY, LBJ: HOW MANY FRIENDS DID YOU MAKE TODAY?"

From Alfred Steinberg's book *Sam Johnson's Boy* we learn of this exchange in 1956 between Senate majority leader LBJ and *Newsweek* reporter Sam Shaffer:

> *"If you want to know what Lyndon Baines Johnson was going to do at the national convention," Johnson screamed, "why didn't you come to Lyndon Baines Johnson and ask him what Lyndon Baines Johnson was going to do?"*
>
> *"All right," said Shaffer, hiding all signs of intimidation, "What is Lyndon Baines Johnson going to do at the convention?"*
>
> *"I don't know," was the answer.*

"Why do you come and ask me,
the leader of the Western world,
a chicken-shit question like that?"

—LBJ,
to a reporter's question he obviously
deemed trivial

TEDDY AND TAFT: A LOVE STORY

They had once been the best of friends. In fact, while Teddy Roosevelt was in office he groomed William Howard Taft to replace him.

When joined by a third friend, Elihu Root, they called themselves "The Three Musketeers." Teddy Roosevelt was D'Artagnan (of course), Taft was Porthos, and Elihu Root was Athos. In reality these three men were perhaps the most powerful men in the world, for Roosevelt was president while Taft and Root were his secretaries of war and state respectively.

Roosevelt and Taft were an unlikely pair of friends. Roosevelt was a man of action, a wound-up cyclotron of energy and excitement, a rugged outdoorsman and soldier who met life head-on and was always headed out the door for a new and grand adventure. Taft, on the other hand, was large (sometimes weighing as much as 330 pounds) and slow

Mr. Taft Writes a Letter

★ ★ ★

- "When I am addressed as 'Mr. President' I turn to see whether you are not at my elbow."
- "I want you to know that I do nothing in the Executive Office without considering what you would do under the same circumstances."
- "I can never forget that the power that I now exercise was a voluntary transfer from you to me."

moving and required so much sleep that his closest aide had learned to cough loudly and wake him when he nodded off during meetings.

Perhaps it was Roosevelt's secret in life, but he always brought out the best in the people around him. His influence over Taft provides the perfect example of this. Taft found Teddy's attention and trust to be flattering and confidence-boosting. He became, you might say, a new man, for he was always eager to please and here now was a man to serve who was so much larger than life—you could even say Teddy was much larger than Taft himself.

With Roosevelt solidly behind him, Taft was easily elected president. However, once in office Taft discovered that no matter how large his feet were, it was not so easy to fill the presidential shoes of Theodore Roosevelt—and when he turned to ask Roosevelt for help, the former president was gone, off to Africa on safari and on other far-flung adventures.

Taft made some mistakes. He did some things that displeased his old friend Teddy. And by the time Teddy Roosevelt returned to the States, the damage was done. From Roosevelt's perspective, Taft had turned his back on what he—as president—had begun. Their friendship ended both bitterly and publicly.

Taft was devastated by the loss. In truth, he had never wanted to be president to begin with. He had only pursued the office to please his ambitious wife, who wanted to be First Lady, and to help his friend Teddy continue to carry out the policies they both believed in.

Meanwhile, an angry Roosevelt decided to run against this former friend for the Republican nomination when it came time for Taft to run for reelection.

The fight for the party's support was bitter, leaving the two ex-friends calling each other names like "weakling," "puzzlewit," and "fathead with the brains of a guinea pig" (Roosevelt of Taft) and "egotist" and "demagogue" (Taft of Roosevelt). Taft eventually won the

Republican Party's nomination, while Roosevelt started his own party to run against him. Ironically, neither won, for the Republican Party split the vote and Democrat Woodrow Wilson won with 41.8 percent of the vote. Roosevelt took second with 27.4 percent, and Taft took third with 23.2 percent.

Taft, of course, was the real loser in more ways than one. Not only had he lost the election, but he had also lost the friend who had helped him grow from cocoon to butterfly.

Years Later, a Hug and a Handshake

Five years later, while checking into Chicago's Blackstone Hotel, Taft was informed by a clerk that Theodore Roosevelt was at that moment upstairs in the restaurant dining alone. Taft made his way to the dining room immediately and, according to William Manners's *TR and Will:*

Looking about, Taft finally located TR at a little table across the room and walked quickly toward him. Intent on his meal though TR was, the sudden stillness in the dining room caused him to look up. He immediately threw down his napkin and rose, his hand extended. They shook hands vigorously and slapped each other on the back. Those in the dining hall cheered, and it was not until then that TR and Will Taft realized that they had an audience and bowed and smiled to it. Then they sat down and chatted for a half hour.

As we say today, closure is a wonderful thing. And for Teddy and Taft, time was of the essence, for Roosevelt died less than a year later.

Taft later expressed his feelings about their reconciliation meeting:

I want to say to you how glad I am that Theodore and I came together after that long painful interval. Had he died in a hostile state of mind toward me, I would have mourned the fact all my life. I loved him always and cherish his memory.

What color was Taft's parachute?

★ ★ ★

After serving as president, Taft went on to the Supreme Court, even becoming chief justice. Ironically, this was really the job he had always wanted; he only ran for president to please Teddy and his own ambitious wife.

As Taft himself once said, "Next to my wife and children, [the Court] is the nearest thing to my heart." And "The truth is that in my present life [as chief justice] I don't remember that I was ever president."

5

MONEY!

*C*ONSIDER THIS:

**Only one president in our nation's history
—Andrew Jackson—
ever paid off the national debt.**

GREED! CORRUPTION! GRAFT!

It's a problem.

On an almost consistent basis over time, those presidents who campaigned the longest and hardest to end corruption in government had the most corrupt administrations.

"Why would that be," you ask?

Theories abound. One suggests that those who scream the loudest about corruption are probably the most corrupt. Others postulate that the presidents who went down in history for having corrupt administrations are those who devoted the most to rooting the corruption out.

INTRODUCING THE KING OF CORRUPTION

The three presidents who made the biggest stink about government corruption were probably Buchanan, Grant, and Truman. Ironically, they also had three of the most corrupt administrations in history.

To be fair, no one has ever pointed a finger at Harry Truman or Ulysses S. Grant and accused them personally of any wrongdoing. In both cases they were upright and honest guys who made the same mistake: They appointed their good buddies from back home to key positions in their administrations—but their buddies were neither qualified to hold those jobs nor did they bring to their jobs the strong moral backbone needed to serve their country without serving themselves (quite liberally and profitably) first.

Corrupt? No.
Just stupid.

★ ★ ★

Chester A. Arthur once sold twenty-six
wagon loads of White House furniture
for a total of eight thousand dollars.
What he apparently didn't know was
that some of the furniture was priceless.

BUCHANAN, ON THE OTHER HAND, WAS A SNAKE

"Next in importance to the maintenance of the Constitution and the Union is the duty of preserving the government free from the taint, or even the suspicion, of corruption."

—FROM THE INAUGURATION SPEECH OF JAMES BUCHANAN

*E*ven before he was elected:

- Buchanan promised lucrative government contracts to friends in exchange for large campaign contributions.
- Supporters in some states arranged for aliens to be illegally naturalized and then transported to the polls.

And after he was elected:

- Buchanan promised to award handsome contracts to a large contributor who gave $16,000 to his campaign.
- A large navy contract was given to a company in Philadelphia that promised to influence the reelection of a close friend of Buchanan's.
- Giant printing contracts were given to another close friend, who then subcontracted them at half the price to printers who made large contributions to the president's election campaign. Printing contracts were also used to twist the arms of various members of Congress—if members voted with the president, the large contracts

How bad could it get, you ask?

★ ★ ★

James Buchanan's administration was so corrupt that given a chance to buy Cuba for only thirty million dollars, Congress voted to pass on the deal because there was a collective fear that Buchanan and his cronies would somehow abscond with the money.

would be awarded to printers in their states or districts.

- The postmaster of New York embezzled $155,000 and fled the country.
- The secretary of war resigned after bilking the government of five million dollars.
- The personal banker of the secretary of war won the right to buy a military reservation in Minnesota.
- The House doorkeeper was found guilty of falsifying accounts and had to resign.

"That's What Friends Are For"

Whether you are talking about Buchanan or Grant or Truman, the finger always gets pointed at the same place: their friends.

Grant and Truman, however, existed on a much higher moral plane. While it's true they made the mistake of putting their no-good friends in high places, they didn't know their friends would repay them by robbing the country blind.

Buchanan, on the other hand, knew exactly what was going on. In fact, in one case Buchanan received a letter suggesting he give a lucrative navy contract to a particular company in Philadelphia that in return promised to help influence the congressional reelection of one of Buchanan's close friends. Buchanan initialed the letter, sent it to the Navy Department, and the Philadelphia firm was awarded the contract.

Ten days later Buchanan's friend won reelection.

Disclaimer: Any similarities between the historical events detailed above and more re-cent events is purely ironic.

Not Even Quicken Could Help

★ ★ ★

As Ulysses S. Grant's presidency showed, he was not terribly good with money. But he was a war hero, and he did have a good name, and that was worth something. After he left the White House he became a partner in the investment house of Grant & Ward—which subsequently failed and left him in dept. Although he had cancer at the time, he put pen to paper and wrote his memoirs to pay off his creditors.

While the book was a huge success and earned more than $450,000, Grant died four days after he finished writing it.

Harding's administration was overrun with corruption as well, but at least he never got on a soapbox about it before taking office. Like Truman and Grant, it was his friends who were on the take, not Harding himself. In fact, when he died, he was deeply in debt.

WHAT'S LOVE GOT TO DO WITH IT?

Bill Clinton needs money. Your money. Bad.

He's the first president in history to be forced to set up a legal defense fund to pay legal bills incurred while in office. He not only needs you to donate money so he can defend himself against charges of sexual harassment, but he and Hillary also need the bucks for the costs associated with the Whitewater probe. And since a bunch of the money already in their defense fund has come from "questionable" sources, they'll probably need even more money to help defray the cost of an investigation into the fund itself.

Ironic, isn't it? A good part of their troubles, at this point, comes from having too many shady, but generous, friends.

As of February 1997, the Clinton defense fund had paid $766,134 of the Clintons' Whitewater and sexual harassment suit legal bills. That still leaves more than $2.3 million in lawyer bills yet unpaid. And that's just the tab so far. As of this writing, Whitewater has not been resolved. The sexual harassment suit has not been resolved. And any investigation into questionable contributions to the defense fund has yet to begin.

Meanwhile, the cost to the Clintons of defending themselves continues to increase at a rate of about $1 million per year.

At a 1996 press conference Bill summed up the situation this way: "I feel badly that twenty years of our hard effort may go away, but if I stay healthy, I'll be able to pay my bills and earn a pretty good living."

"It's the Economy, Stupid"

*L*et's face it, dealing with money is half the job. Chances are that's why Jimmy Carter didn't get reelected.

And, short of getting lucky, there's only one way to win the money game when you're president: You've got to have great financial advisers.

The funny thing about Carter is that if he wanted good economic advice, he didn't have to look any farther than his own daughter. After all, while he was running for president in 1976, she set herself up with her own booming business right on the Georgia governor's mansion lawn.

Had Jimmy used the same simple techniques to run the government that Amy used out on the lawn, the country might not have been saddled with skyrocketing inflation and prime interest rates in the range of 20 percent during his term in office.

But at least, we presume, Carter is doing better with his own finances—unlike Thomas Jefferson, James Monroe, Andrew Jackson, Ulysses S. Grant, and Warren Harding. All four of these guys were so bad at managing their own money they died poor and (with the exception of Jefferson) in debt.

DID AMY CARTER LEARN ABOUT $$$ FROM LBJ?

LBJ made his first forage into the world of business when he opened Johnson's Shoe Shine Shop inside Cecil Maddox's barbershop. For the first few weeks the business ran fine, in part thanks to Cecil's existing customer base and the ads LBJ ran in the local paper. But then disaster struck: LBJ's father shut the business down because he didn't think it was any way for a nine-year-old to spend his time.

While her father was running for president, Amy Carter was outside with friends selling lemonade to tourists and members of the press. Initially, the price was a nickel, but Amy soon realized the market could bear a price increase.

So she raised the price to a dime. Yet business was still booming, so the three young entrepreneurs expanded and added new products to their line: three varieties of sandwiches and Frisbee rentals. The business was suddenly closed, however, when the Secret Service declared it a potential security risk.

FOR LOVE OR MONEY

While a young man, JFK appeared at a rally for candidates who were running for the Massachusetts legislature. He waited patiently as candidate after candidate went before the audience and spoke—and he noticed a similarity in the stories each of them told.

When his turn finally came to address the assembly he began: "I seem to be the only person here tonight who didn't come up the hard way!"

While life for Kennedy was relatively easy in his younger years, the same was not true for all of our presidents. Some, in fact, had to do some pretty odd things to make ends meet before making it into the Oval Office.

PRESIDENT: **George Washington**

JOB: During his first year as president he ran a ferry service back and forth across the Potomac.

PRESIDENT: **Thomas Jefferson**

JOB: Given a choice, he once said, he would have rather been a gardener than president. He imported plants from other countries to study them, and while conventional wisdom of the time said tomatoes were poisonous, he grew and ate them for dinner. He was also an inventor and was responsible for the development of the dumb waiter, the lazy Susan, an automatic closing door the design of which is still—fundamentally—in use on buses today, the revolving chair, the folding chair, and a machine that enabled him to make a duplicate copy of a letter as he wrote it. He was also an inventive chef and created both Baked Alaska and Chicken à la King (which George Washington loved!).

PRESIDENT: **John Quincy Adams**

JOB: Okay, he didn't exactly come up the hard way, either, but at age fourteen he was made private secretary to the American envoy to Russia, and at fifteen he was secretary to the American emissaries negotiating peace with England. In addition, he is the only president to be a published poet.

PRESIDENT: **Zachary Taylor**

JOB: He was a career military man. Before being elected president he spent most of his adult life fighting Indians and the Mexican Army during the Mexican-American War. Funny thing was, he was a very short war hero, so he needed someone to give him a boost every time he got up on his horse.

PRESIDENT: **James Buchanan**

JOB: He was once a prizefighter.

PRESIDENT: **Grover Cleveland**

JOB: In the span of just three and a half years he was the mayor of Buffalo, New York, the governor of the state of New York and the president of the United States. Before becoming mayor of Buffalo he was the sheriff of Erie County, New York, and was called upon twice to spring the trap at a hanging—thus making him the only president in history with the job of hangman on his résumé.

PRESIDENT: **William McKinley**

JOB: He drove a coffee wagon out to soldiers on the battlefield during the Civil War. His commanding officer was Rutherford B. Hayes.

PRESIDENT: **Teddy Roosevelt**

JOB: He spent several years working as a cowboy in the Dakota Badlands—and after he rounded up a gang of rustlers, he wore the badge of a deputy sheriff.

PRESIDENT: **Warren G. Harding**

JOB: He was a newspaper man . . . and a poker player. In fact, he won controlling interest in the *Marion Daily Star,* his local newspaper, in a card game.

> As Harding used to say at his weekly poker game: "Forget that I'm president of the United States. I'm Warren Harding, playing poker with friends, and I'm going to beat hell out of them." (And when he was short of cash, he would ante up by putting pieces of White House china into the pot.)

PRESIDENT: **Herbert Hoover**

JOB: Hoover was an orphan, and his first job was picking bugs off potato plants—for which he was paid a dollar per hundred (bugs, that is, not plants).

His first job out of college was as a mine worker—for seventy hours a week he pushed an ore cart in a California gold mine. Then, using what he learned while getting a degree in mining engineering from Stanford, he went on to become a millionaire.

But everything Hoover touched didn't turn to gold. In fact, he aspired to be a political writer and wrote many books containing his views and commentary on the state of the world . . . that no one wanted to read.

On the other hand, he did write two books that did rather well. The first, which he wrote twenty-one years before he became president, was called *Principles of Mining*. In fact, it became the definitive text for mining engineering students until it went out of print almost sixty years later. His second success as an author? It was *Fishing for Fun and to Wash Your Soul*, which he wrote thirty-three years after leaving the White House.

PRESIDENT: Harry Truman

JOB: After World War I he opened a haberdashery in Kansas City with a friend. Three years later they were broke.

PRESIDENT: LBJ

JOB: He worked on a road gang after high school. Later he put himself through college by working as the college janitor and picking up trash on campus.

PRESIDENT: **Richard Nixon**

JOB: He spent his summers working as a carnival barker for the Wheel of Chance at the Slippery Gulch Rodeo. Later he owned the only hamburger stand in the South Pacific, Nixon's Snack Shack, during World War II.

> "I have often thought that if there had been a good rap group around in those days, I would have chosen a career in music instead of politics."
>
> —RICHARD NIXON

PRESIDENT: **Jimmy Carter**

JOB: Flew blimps for the navy.

PRESIDENT: **Gerald Ford**

JOB: As a college senior he was recruited to play for the Detroit Lions and the Green Bay Packers—but he decided to go to law school instead. While at Yale Law School he worked as an assistant football coach, a boxing instructor, and a magazine model. He also worked as a forest ranger at Yellowstone National Park. His chief duties: directing traffic and feeding the bears.

PRESIDENT: **Ronald Reagan**

JOB: According to Reagan, he saved the lives of seventy-seven people as a boy when he worked as lifeguard at the river near his family home in Dixon, Illinois.

PRESIDENT: **George Bush**

JOB: His first job after he left the navy was on the Texas oilfields. His responsibilities included painting machinery and sweeping floors.

PRESIDENT: **Bill Clinton**

JOB: Clinton's first boss was his grandfather, who owned Cassidy's General Store in Hope, Arkansas. Bill's job was to greet customers with a smile and a hearty handshake as they came through the door of the store.

DOES CRIME PAY?

After Gerald Ford granted Richard Nixon a full pardon for any crimes he may have committed in relationship to Watergate, he then lobbied Congress to pay Nixon $850,000 to cover his expenses while making the transition from the presidency to civilian life.

The sum of $850,000 was considered to be a compromise deal since The Presidential Transition Act of 1963 provides ex-presidents who complete their full term in office with one million dollars to cover their expenses during this six-month transition period.

In a compromise deal of its own, Congress agreed to pay Nixon two hundred thousand dollars for his transition expenses.

Presidents who were never lawyers or never studied law:

★ ★ ★

- George Washington
- William Henry Harrison
- Zachary Taylor
- Ulysses S. Grant
- Woodrow Wilson
- Warren G. Harding
- Herbert Hoover
- Dwight Eisenhower
- JFK
- LBJ
- Jimmy Carter
- Ronald Reagan

A Few Good Men . . .

- **G**eorge Washington refused to accept his salary as president.
- Herbert Hoover and JFK both took the money and donated it to charity.
- When Eddie Cantor and the Lone Ranger asked the children of America to each send a dime to the president to help the March of Dimes—of which FDR was the founder and chairman—so many dimes were sent to the White House (sometimes as many as 150,000 a day) that fifty extra postal workers had to be hired to handle the increased volume. In total, more than three million dimes were received.

. . . One Stinker . . .

*I*n 1991 *Spy* magazine reported that it cost the Secret Service three million dollars a year to protect the life of former President Gerald Ford and that the government was also spending $420,000 a year to maintain his office.

Meanwhile, Ford was leveraging his role as chief executive for every dollar he could get.

Consider this: When Ford turned the White House over to Jimmy Carter in 1977 his net worth was about $250,000. Just a few years later, after allowing a variety of companies ranging from American Express to Commercial Credit to Spectradyne (the company that pumps pay-per-view movies, including porn, into many hotels) buy him for as much as $140,000 a year each, he was a millionaire.

Okay, "buy him" is a bit harsh. Let's say they paid him to be a *consultant* or a member of the board of directors. He got the dough (as much as $1.7 million a year in the late 1980s)—they got the prestige. So, to the degree that Ford is still cutting these kinds of deals, he now supports himself the same way Michael Jordan does.

Not a bad deal for a guy who was appointed vice president when Spiro Agnew resigned, who succeeded to the presidency when Richard Nixon resigned, and who then lost to Jimmy Carter when he ran for reelection. (In other words, unless you're from his home state of Michigan, this is one president you never had a chance to elect.)

But here's the rub: In 1993 Congress voted to stop funding the offices of former presidents by 1998, although they'll still receive an annual pension equal to that of a cabinet secretary (currently more than $140,000/year) and Secret Service protection for life.

His Just Reward

★ ★ ★

Isn't it an amazing coincidence that FDR also happens to be pictured on the dime?

No coincidence at all, as it turns out. In fact, after FDR died in 1945, Congress voted to commemorate the work he did on behalf of the March of Dimes by putting his profile on the coin.

Ford, however, who continues to make a fortune by lending his name to those who can afford to pay for it, is lobbying Congress to push that cutoff date farther into the future so he can stay on the U.S. government gravy train for as long as humanly possible.

... AND ONE GUY WHO WASN'T TOO BRIGHT

James Monroe entered politics at the age of twenty-four and worked in public service for the rest of his life. He was a member of the Virginia Assembly and the Continental Congress, a senator, a minister to France, the governor of Virginia, secretary of state, and president for two terms. He was a man truly devoted to his country.

Only one problem. For many of the forty-nine years he spent as a public servant, he spent more than he earned. Therefore, when he retired in 1825 after his second term as president, he was broke. So he did the only logical thing: He turned to the government for a handout.

His rationale was that if he served his country for close to fifty years and had less money than he started with, then much of the money he spent on the expenses of being a public servant must have been his own. Therefore, didn't it seem reasonable that he should be reimbursed?

It took them seven years to do it, but Congress finally reimbursed Monroe thirty thousand dollars—just a fraction of what Monroe claimed to have spent. Not that it mattered. By the time Congress made the decision, Monroe had sold off all his land to pay his debts and had gone to live with his daughter and son-in-law. He died shortly afterward.

"JUST PUT IT IN YOUR POCKET!"

For what it's worth, presidential salaries through the ages:

1789 - 1873

George Washington through
the first term of Ulysses S. Grant $25,000/year

1873 - 1909

Grant's second term through
the final term of Teddy Roosevelt $55,000/year

1909 - 1949

William Howard Taft's term through
Harry Truman's first term . . . .$75,000/year (taxable)

1949 - 1969

Harry Truman's second term through
LBJ's final term . . . .$100,000/year (taxable)

1969 - PRESENT

Richard Nixon's first term
to Clinton's current term . . . .$200,000/year (taxable)

The office also comes with certain perks:

- one million dollars per year in discretionary funds the president can use for things like personal aides and other services he deems necessary
- one hundred thousand dollars a year for traveling expenses (which seems kind of ironic since this is for expenses above and beyond the cost of *Air Force One*—of which there are two and both of which cost $40,243 per hour of flight to run—the helicopter *Marine One*—of which there are eight—a motorcade of bulletproof limos, and an army of Secret Service agents, all of which cost millions per year)
- a twelve-thousand-dollar entertainment budget (for those times when he wants to rent a video and invite other world leaders over for a casual evening, perhaps?)
- a nice large staff—for the first 150 years we had a president, if he wanted an assistant he had to pay for it himself. In many cases he would hire a nephew or other family member to help out. Then, in 1939, things changed—Congress kicked in enough money for the president to hire six aides. By the end of World War II (1945) that number had grown to forty-five; by the time Eisenhower left office (1961) it had grown to four hundred; and by the time Nixon left office (1974) there was money for six hundred presidential aides.
- one million dollars to cover the transitional costs of his first six months out of office (in addition to his pension and Secret Service protection for life)

6

PROPHECY!

"If anybody really wanted to shoot the president of the United States, it is not a very difficult job— all one has to do is get on a high building some day with a telescopic rifle and there is nothing anyone can do to defend against such an attempt."

—JFK, THREE HOURS BEFORE HE WAS ASSASSINATED

MORE KENNEDY PROPHECY

> **"Dallas is a very dangerous place. I wouldn't go there. Don't you go."**
> —SENATOR WILLIAM J. FULBRIGHT TO JFK

JFK's favorite poem:
"I Have a Rendevous with Death" by Alan Seeger

One of Jackie Kennedy's first jobs out of college was as the *Washington Times-Herald*'s "Inquiring Photographer." Below are three of the questions she asked Washington celebrities, politicians, and people on the street:

- "If you had a date with Marilyn Monroe, what would you talk about?"
- "Should a candidate's wife campaign with her husband?"
- "What prominent person's death affected you most?"

WEIRD LINCOLN PROPHECY

"You will win the election and will be elected for a second term. But I fear . . . you may not survive your second four years in the White House."

—MARY TODD LINCOLN TO HER HUSBAND, ABE, AFTER HE WAS NOMINATED
FOR PRESIDENT FOR THE FIRST TIME BUT BEFORE HE WAS ELECTED

"I believe there are men who want to take my life. And I have no doubt they will do it."

—ABRAHAM LINCOLN, HOURS BEFORE HE WAS SHOT

- *A*braham Lincoln was the first president ever to be photographed at his inauguration. Eerily, in one photo he stands near the man who would later assassinate him, John Wilkes Booth.
- Abe Lincoln's young son Robert was waiting for a train one day when the crowd on the platform surged forward to meet the incoming train. Robert lost his footing and began to slip between the platform and the moving train . . . until a hand reached out and grabbed him, saving his life. The helping hand belonged to the famous actor Edwin Wilkes Booth. Unbeknown to Booth or the young boy whose life he just saved, Booth's brother would later shoot and kill the boy's father.

> **"It has been advertized that we will be there and I cannot disappoint the people. Otherwise I would not go. I do not want to go. Good-bye, Crook."**
>
> —ABE'S LAST WORDS TO WHITE HOUSE GUARD COLONEL WILLIAM CROOK
>
> (LINCOLN'S LAST TWO WORDS CONFUSED CROOK UNTIL LATER IN THE EVENING WHEN HE HEARD THE PRESIDENT HAD BEEN SHOT; THE PRESIDENT'S CUSTOMARY SALUTATION TO CROOK WHEN HE WAS GOING OUT FOR THE EVENING WAS "GOOD NIGHT.")

- Robert Lincoln is the only man in the history of the United States known to have witnessed the assassinations of three different presidents—his father, Abraham Lincoln; James Garfield, and William McKinley. After he saw anarchist Leon Czolgosz shoot McKinley, Robert Lincoln vowed he would never again appear in public with an incumbent president.

> **"They won't think anything of it."**
>
> —ABRAHAM LINCOLN'S LAST WORDS, IN RESPONSE TO MRS. LINCOLN'S QUESTION AS TO WHETHER HE THOUGHT THE AUDIENCE AT FORD'S THEATRE WOULD MIND IF THEY HELD HANDS WHILE WATCHING THE PERFORMANCE

PRESIDENTIAL DESTINY

There goes life imitating art again.

At one point Ronald Reagan was considered for the role of Rick in the film *Casablanca* (translation: "White House"). And before they were married he and Nancy Reagan appeared in the General Electric Theatre production of *A Turkey for President.*

> **"I wish for you that you may never be president."**
> **—GROVER CLEVELAND TO FIVE-YEAR-OLD FDR**

William Henry Harrison promised voters that if elected he wouldn't run for another term. How prophetic—he died thirty-one days after taking office.

"How can you argue with that?"

★ ★ ★

Richard Nixon was a high school and college debate champion. In fact, his team at Whittier College once won twenty-seven straight matches.

"He was so good it kind of disturbed me," his debate coach once remarked. "He had this ability to kind of slide around an argument, instead of meeting it head-on."

"Mother, I would like to become a lawyer—an honest lawyer, one who can't be bought by crooks."
—YOUNG RICHARD NIXON TO HIS MOTHER

"The best potato masher a mother could wish for."
—HANNAH NIXON, ABOUT HER SON RICHARD

LBJ started telling people he was going to be president when he was in the first grade. His first real presidential experience was his election to the office of president of his high school senior class. Whether or not he won the election on merit can be argued, however—it turns out no one else in his graduating class of six wanted the job.

When Dwight D. Eisenhower and his brother, Edgar, graduated high school, their yearbook predicted Edgar would grow up to be president of the United States—and Dwight would someday be a history teacher.

"The convention will be deadlocked, and after the other candidates have gone their limit, some twelve or fifteen men, worn out and bleary-eyed for lack of sleep, will sit down, about two o'clock in the morning, around a table in a smoke-filled room in some hotel, and decide the nomination. When that time comes, Harding will be selected."

—A FRIGHTENINGLY ACCURATE PREDICTION BY WARREN HARDING'S CAMPAIGN MANAGER, HARRY DAUGHERTY

"I Changed My Mind"

While Harry Truman was president, it became obvious the White House needed major renovation work done after Harry, and the bathtub in which he was soaking, almost fell through the floor and into the middle of a reception Bess was holding for the Daughters of the American Revolution.

While it was true the house did need a new foundation, reinforced beams and steel framing, fireproofing, the addition of air conditioning, and the latest in communications technology, it was Truman's idea to add a balcony to the second floor of the South Portico so he and his family and their guests could sit outside and enjoy Washington's evening breezes.

Truman, however, didn't anticipate the expense of the balcony project or the controversy and problems the addition would create, especially for the Treasury Department. After all, there were millions of twenty-dollar bills in circulation that showed the White House without a balcony, and what on earth were they going to do about that?

But Truman put his foot down, got his way, and got his balcony. He and his family moved out of the White House for twenty-seven months, living across the street at Blair House while the executive mansion could be gutted and rebuilt.

Here's the punch line of the story: Two days after the White House project was complete Harry Truman announced he wouldn't seek reelection.

LINCOLN-KENNEDY COINCIDENCES?

You've heard it before:

- Both had seven letters in their last names, both were over six feet tall, and both were athletic.
- Both were shot in the head on a Friday, and both were seated beside their wives when shot.
- Lincoln was shot at Ford's Theatre, and Kennedy was shot in a Lincoln limo, which is made by Ford.
- Lincoln was in Box 7 at Ford's Theatre, and Kennedy was in Car 7 of the Dallas motorcade.
- In both cases, the assassin had three names with fifteen letters: John Wilkes Booth and Lee Harvey Oswald.
- Booth shot Lincoln in a theater and was captured at a warehouse. Oswald shot Kennedy from a warehouse and was captured in a theater.
- Kennedy's secretary, Evelyn Lincoln (whose husband's nickname was Abe), told him not to go to Dallas. Some say Lincoln had a secretary named John Kennedy who told him not to go to the theater.
- Both were elected to the U.S. House of Representatives for the first time in '46, were runners-up for their party's nomination for vice president in '56, and were elected president in '60.
- Both were succeeded by southern Democrats named Johnson.

The list goes on and on, and it's interesting stuff, but so what? They both had two hands, two feet, and two eyes too. They both put on their pants one foot at a time, and they both . . . Well, you get the idea.

The bottom line of the Lincoln-Kennedy coincidences is this: You can think about them all day long, and all you'll have at dinner time is a creepy feeling and an urge to watch *X-Files* reruns all night.

On the other hand, if you take the time to delve into the not-so-eerie similarities between the Kennedy and Adams (as in John and John Quincy) families, you might just learn something about yourself, your own family, and even the world around you. And that, in our opinion, is a day's work worth doing.

"Just as I went into politics because Joe [Jr.] died, if anything happened to me tomorrow, my brother Bobby would run for my seat in the Senate. And if Bobby died, Teddy would take over for him."

—JFK

"The world is tired of us."

—BROOKS ADAMS, GREAT-GRANDSON OF JOHN ADAMS

THE INFAMOUS KENNEDY FAMILY

Joseph (Joe) Patrick Kennedy Sr. was one of the richest men in the country in the '20s and '30s. First he was a bank president. Tiring of that, he went to Hollywood to make movies (and have an affair with Gloria Swanson). Tiring of that, he moved on to become FDR's chairman of the Securities and Exchange Commission (SEC) and then ambassador to England. At this point, he began to have his own aspirations toward the presidency. His dream, however, was thwarted as FDR ran for a third and fourth term. That was when Joe Kennedy decided if he couldn't be president, at least one of his sons would be.

Joe Kennedy Senior Had Four Sons

Joe Jr. was the heir apparent of his father's wish to be president. The elder Kennedy pushed all of his sons to play hard, to ignore pain and risk and danger, and to win at all costs—but he pushed Joe Jr. the hardest. Joe Jr., after all, had the toughest job of all ahead of him: winning the presidency. Tragically, after flying fifty missions as a navy pilot during World War II and receiving his orders home, Joe Jr. volunteered to fly one last mission as the pilot of an experimental airplane. The plane exploded in midair, and Joe Jr.'s body was never found. Why did he agree to that final flight—one that was acknowledged to be dangerous—when he could have been on his way home instead? Some have suggested that he was driven by the fierce competitive spirit instilled in him by his father. After all, his younger brother John (JFK) had already won a Purple Heart.

John Fitzgerald inherited his father's dream. And with JFK, Joe Sr. finally realized that dream. However, we all know the ending to that chapter: After winning the presidency in 1960, JFK was assassinated in 1963.

Robert was JFK's attorney general and had just won the California Democratic Party's presidential primary for the 1968 election when he was assassinated. Like his brother John, he seemed to relish taking risks—even after his brother was assassinated, he ignored the warnings of friends and family and even the Secret Service and would rush out into crowds unprotected.

Ted was the only one left. Many predicted he could have won the Democratic Party's nomination for president in 1972 . . . until he drove his car off the side of a bridge, managed to free himself, claimed to have dived back down into the water to save his passenger, then went on to the party they had been headed to to get help. He did not call the police until the next day.

It was assumed that Bobby or Ted would eventually capture the presidency again for the Kennedy clan, and if not one of them, then one of the next generation's sons. Instead, the third generation of Kennedys is beginning to look more and more like its dynastical predecessors, the Adams family:

- Robert's son David died of a drug overdose.
- Robert's son Robert Jr. was arrested for possession of heroin in 1983; he was working as an assistant district attorney at the time.
- Ted's daughter, Kara, was in and out of halfway houses in the 1970s as she fought an addiction to drugs.
- Ted's son Ted Jr. was once arrested for possession of marijuana.

- Christopher Kennedy Lawford was arrested in 1980 for attempting to impersonate a doctor so he could buy the prescription drug Darvon; later that year he was arrested again when he tried to buy some heroin.
- Robert S. Shriver was busted in the early seventies for possessing marijuana.
- Jean Kennedy Smith's son, William Kennedy Smith, became very famous very fast when he was accused of rape. He was acquitted but ran into the law again when he popped a club bouncer in the nose and was arrested for assault and battery.
- Michael Kennedy, RFK's son, is the most recent Kennedy to make the news. His December '97 death in a freak skiing accident is the unfortunate end to recent allegations of a five-year affair with the family's nineteen-year-old baby-sitter.

Who's Who in the Kennedy Clan?

There're so darn many of them, it's hard to keep them straight.

Joe Sr. and Rose Kennedy had nine children: Rosemary, Joe Jr., Kathleen, JFK, Eunice, Patricia, RFK, Jean, and Ted. These nine Kennedy children in turn had twenty-nine kids of their own:

- JFK and Jackie Bouvier Kennedy had two kids: Caroline and John.
- Eunice Kennedy Shriver and Sargent Shriver had five children: Robert, Maria, Timothy, Mark, and Anthony.
- Patricia Kennedy Lawford and Peter Lawford had four children: Christopher, Sydney, Victoria, and Robin.

- RFK and Ethel Skatel Kennedy had eleven kids: Kathleen, Joe II, Robert Jr., David, Mary Courtney, Michael, Mary Kerry, Chris, Matthew, Douglas, and Rory.
- Jean Kennedy Smith and Stephen Smith had four children: Stephen Jr., William, Amanda, and Kym.
- Ted Kennedy and Joan Bennett Kennedy had three children: Kara, Edward Jr., and Patrick.

THE ADAMS FAMILY

The Adamses were the first family to view the presidency as a crown or an honor to be handed down from one generation to the next. However, unlike the Kennedys, who often seemed to suffer from a rather grand view of themselves, many members of the Adams family suffered from the affliction of depression.

John Adams was the first vice president of the United States and the second president—but he didn't relate well with the public and wasn't very popular. In fact, he was the first president to run for a second term and not be reelected. (Ironically, his son John Quincy was the second president to run for reelection and be denied a second term by the voting public.)

President John Adams Had Three Sons

John Quincy, who became as unpopular a president as his father, suffered from manic-depression.

Charles, who died the ugly and lonely death of an alcoholic in a run-down apartment in New York City.

Thomas, who also died as a result of his alcoholism.

John Adams's Son John Quincy Also Had Three Sons

George Washington Adams, who John Quincy and his wife, Louisa, expected to become president, instead suffered from horrible anxiety attacks and paranoia (much as his father and grandfather did). An alcoholic and drug addict as well, he killed himself just after his twenty-eighth birthday.

John II was encouraged to pursue an interest in public service but was also trained to run the Adams family mills. As the mills went bankrupt under his watch he drank more and more until he finally died at thirty-one from a variety of alcohol-related causes.

Charles Francis was also expected to go into some avenue of public service and in fact was elected to the same seat in the House of Representatives his father (John Quincy Adams) had held for seventeen years after serving as president. Charles Francis later ran for governor of Massachusetts, but lost.

Charles Francis Had Five Sons
(Two of Whom Are Worth Noting Here)

Son Henry was both a history professor at Harvard and a successful author. Like many others in his family, he, too, suffered from tremendous periods of depression, compounded by the fact that his wife committed suicide.

Brooks, like his brother, was also a historian and a writer and also suffered from depression. He was the last of the Adams family to die. Shortly before his death he wrote: "It is not full four generations since John Adams wrote the constitution of Massachusetts. It is time that we perished. The world is tired of us."

JOHN ADAMS: A FIRM BELIEVER IN BIG GOVERNMENT

If John Adams had had his way, our government would have been more of a monarchy. For instance, he thought many of the positions of power in the new government should be handed down from generation to generation within families. And instead of calling our leader "President of the United States," he preferred a more robust title—something like "His Highness, the President of the United States and Protector of Their Liberties" ("His Highness" for short). How much of this was motivated by the fact he figured he was next in line for the job is not known. But it is known he and Thomas Jefferson didn't get along—while Adams was a firm believer in big government, Jefferson believed "government is best which governs least."

A Family of Bad Sports

John Adams was the first president to run for reelection and lose to his challenger. He was such a bad loser that he didn't even stick around long enough to attend his challenger's inauguration.

The second president to run for reelection and lose was John Adams's son John Quincy. Like his father, he, too, was a sore loser and left town without attending the inauguration of his opponent.

WILLIAM MCKINLEY DEMONSTRATES WHY YOU SHOULD NEVER TEMPT FATE

William McKinley always wore a red carnation in his lapel for good luck. No matter what.

One day, in an act that was completely uncharacteristic of him, President McKinley took off his lucky flower and offered it to a little girl he spotted in the crowd surrounding him.

Moments later, an assassin shot him. Eighty days later he was dead.

THE MARTHA STEWART OF ASSASSINS

While waiting for a train at the B&O station in Washington, James Garfield was shot and killed by an anarchist named Charles Guiteau.

Guiteau shot Garfield in the back using a five-barrel, .44-caliber pistol called a British Bulldog. Guiteau claimed he chose the gun for a very good reason: He thought it would look really good on display in a museum someday.

Guess the joke was on Guiteau; more than a hundred years after he shot the president, no one in Washington has a clue as to where his fancy gun might be—not the Smithsonian, not the National Archive, not the FBI's weapon collection in Washington, not even the U.S. Attorney's office, which prosecuted the case.

On the other hand, other pieces of memorabilia associated with the assassination are easy to put one's finger on; for instance, the National Museum of Heath and Medicine at Walter Reed Army Medical Center in Washington, D.C., has Guiteau's skeleton (but not the skull), what is left of his brain (part of it was removed for medical study), and, for some strange reason, his spleen. The museum also has three of Garfield's vertebrae that were struck by Guiteau's bullet.

But, alas, Guiteau's showcase pistol is nowhere to be found.

Actual Performance May Vary

★ ★ ★

"You may write down in your books now the largest percentage of blunders which you think I will be likely to make, and you will be sure to find in the end that I have made many more than you have calculated, many more."

—James Garfield

Not!

"We in America today are nearer to the final triumph over poverty than ever before in the history of any land. The poorhouse is vanishing from among us. We have not yet reached the goal but, given a chance to go forward with the policies of the last eight years, we shall soon with the help of God be in sight of the day when poverty will be banished from this nation."

—Herbert Hoover,
upon accepting the Republican nomination for president in 1928.
Less than a year later the stock market crashed and the nation was
plunged into the darkness of the Great Depression.

Poor, Poor Herbert Hoover

★ ★ ★

The guy was so desperate to end the Depression he began grasping at straws for a solution, no matter how ridiculous. Case in point: He offered pop singer Rudy Vallee a medal if only the singer would "sing a song that would make people forget their troubles and the Depression."

WALK SOFTLY AND CARRY A BIG SUPERSTITION

- Woodrow Wilson was superstitious about the number thirteen—there were thirteen letters in his name and thirteen original colonies when the United States was founded—and he believed it was his lucky number. Therefore, when once sailing from the United States to Europe for a peace conference, he made sure the ship slowed down so he wouldn't arrive on the twelfth but on the thirteenth instead.
- Neither FDR and his family nor Herbert Hoover and his family would ever sit at a table set for thirteen guests. Additionally, FDR refused to travel of a Friday and would never allow himself to be third on a single match.

Prophecy!

- Ronald Reagan believes knocking on wood brings good luck.
- Warren Harding, a career newspaper man, always carried a printer's rule in his vest pocket for good luck.
- Ulysses S. Grant had a thing about retracing his footsteps; anytime he inadvertantly passed his intended destination, he would never turn around and go back exactly the way he came but would take another route, even if it meant he would have to travel far out of his way. You might think this was a charming little neurosis—unless you were on a battlefield under General Grant's command and it was time to retreat.

DEATH!

"Boys, if you ever pray, pray for me now."
—ONE OF HARRY TRUMAN'S FIRST STATEMENTS
TO THE PRESS, AFTER BEING SWORN IN AS PRESIDENT
FOLLOWING THE DEATH OF FDR

"HELLO . . . MR. PRESIDENT?"

EVER WONDER WHAT GOES ON BEHIND THE SCENES when the president dies? Here's how James David Barber, in his book *Presidential Character,* reported on the transfer of presidential power to Harry Truman following FDR's death:

> *The President's death caught [Vice President] Truman entirely by surprise. On April 11, 1945, Harry was his usual ebullient self. When the Senate adjourned that day the reporters flocked around him; one called him "Mr. President," as Senators address their presiding officer. Truman flashed a smile and said, "Boys, those are fighting words out in Missouri where I come from. You'd better smile when you say that! . . ."*
>
> *The next day he whiled away the afternoon on the rostrum writing a newsy letter home, telling his folks to be sure to tune in when, tomorrow night, he would make a speech and introduce the President. At 5:10 he strolled over to Sam Rayburn's "Board of Education" hideaway in the House end of the Capitol where Rayburn's friends often gathered at the end of the day to open a bottle and "strike a blow for liberty." Rayburn gave him the message to call the White House immediately. "Please come right over," he was told, "and come in through the main Pennsylvania entrance."*
>
> *His face turned white. "Holy General Jackson!" he said, raced back to his office, found his chauffeur, and made it to the White House at 5:25, where he was immediately directed to Mrs. Roosevelt's study.*

"Harry," Eleanor said, "the President is dead."

Truman was stunned into silence. Finally he choked out, "Is there anything I can do for you?"

Eleanor replied, "Is there anything we can do for you? For you are the one in trouble now."

The next day, Truman's first as president, was Friday the thirteenth of April.

"SO HELP ME GOD"

In his book *Madmen and Geniuses,* Sol Barzman sets the stage for the death of Warren G. Harding and the swearing in of Calvin Coolidge.

In late July he [Harding] suffered a collapse in Seattle and was moved to San Francisco, where he died in a few days, apparently of a heart attack. The date was August 2, 1923; Harding was fifty-five.

The vice president, in the meantime, had taken his family to his birthplace in Plymouth Notch, Vermont, for a summer vacation. They were staying at his father's farmhouse, which had neither electricity nor a telephone.

It was not until midnight, when the Coolidges had already been asleep for some hours, that an excited messenger came chugging up in an ancient automobile with the news that the president was dead. While oil lamps were lit, and reporters and neighbors gathered, the vice president calmly dressed in a dark suit, came downstairs, and prepared to take the oath of office as the thirtieth president of the United States.

In a room with faded wallpaper, a threadbare rug, and an oil lamp for illumination, the elderly Coolidge, who was a notary public, became the first and only father ever to swear in his own son as president.

When the last phrase of the oath was spoken, the new president solemnly placed his hand on the Bible and spoke the final words with fitting sincerity:

"So help me God."

A few minutes later, he returned upstairs, went back to bed, and fell asleep almost at once.

It's interesting to note that Harding was soon to be up for reelection, and he had no intention of asking Calvin Coolidge to run again as his running mate.

"WHO'S IN CHARGE HERE?"

*A*ccording to Article II, Section I of the Constitution, when the president is no longer able to serve, the vice president shall inherit his job.

But should he?

This particular passage of the Constitution reads:

> *In Case of Removal of the President from Office, or of his Death, Resignation, or Inability to discharge the Powers and Duties of the said Office, the Same shall devolve on the Vice President.*

John Tyler was the first vice president to gain the office of the presidency as a result of the death of the president, when William Henry Harrison died a month after taking office. Unfortunately for Tyler, this also meant it was the first time the above passage of the Constitution was put to the test.

While some agreed with Tyler's interpretation—that he should automatically assume the job of president—others (like John Quincy Adams) argued that the vice president should gain the "Powers and Duties" of the office but not the office itself.

The difference?

Tyler insisted he should become president while his detractors insisted that he merely fulfill the duties of president without receiving the title. The problem arose over the wording of the Constitution, with Tyler interpreting the word "Same" to apply to the "same Office" while his detractors argued that *Same* referred only to the president's "Powers and Duties."

This controversy led to some interesting situations—one of which may have inspired the movie *Miracle on 34th Street.* Just as in the movie Santa's existence is proven by the ability of the postal service to deliver mail to him, whenever mail was sent to the White House addressed to "Acting President" or some variation of that theme, Tyler would return it unopened.

Tyler's detractors were many, for he was elected to the position of vice president as a Whig, inherited the presidency a month after taking office, and then so outraged the Whig Party with his policies that they actually kicked him out of the Party—while he was still president!

Furthermore, those who disagreed with Tyler's interpretation of the Constitution on the issue of the vice president's succession to the presidency were sufficiently outraged with him to begin taking steps to rectify the situation. Thus Tyler became not only the first vice president to succeed to the presi-

---

Just don't accuse him of being a White House intern.

★ ★ ★

Rumor has it that when a messenger arrived at Tyler's house to tell him President Harrison had died, he was on his hands and knees on the floor playing marbles.

dency but also the first to face possible impeachment. (The drive for impeachment didn't have enough supporters in Congress, however, and no resolution to begin impeachment proceedings was ever passed.) As if all this wasn't enough, as the sitting president Tyler suffered the ultimate humiliation of receiving no presidential nomination from either party in the election of 1844.

This vein of controversy followed Tyler to his grave. When he died there was no official recognition of his death or his service to his country by the federal government, a sharp contrast to how the government had treated the deaths of other former presidents. Although Tyler died in 1862, it wasn't until 1911 that the federal government recognized his service by appropriating ten thousand dollars for the building of a memorial in his name. At the dedication of that memorial in 1915, only five senators and five members of the House of Representatives were in attendance.

At least he didn't call it "Whitewater."

★ ★ ★

While president, Tyler bought an estate in Charles City County, Virginia, called "Creek Plantation." He changed the name of the estate to "Sherwood Forest" because, as he explained, he felt like a political outlaw.

"Here lies the body of my good horse 'The General.' For twenty years he bore me around the circuit of my practice and in all that time he never made a blunder. Would that his master could say the same."

—The inscription on John Tyler's horse's grave

"I'M IN CHARGE NOW!"

—SECRETARY OF STATE ALEXANDER HAIG, INCORRECTLY
ASSUMING POWER OF THE UNITED STATES GOVERNMENT
JUST MOMENTS AFTER RONALD REAGAN WAS SHOT

So let's get this straight for General Haig and anyone else who is confused over who succeeds the president should he die or become unable to fulfill the duties of his job.

If the President Dies

The following order dictates who will serve as acting president until the end of the current term:

1. vice president
2. Speaker of the House
3. president pro tempore of the Senate
4. secretary of state
5. secretary of the treasury
6. secretary of defense
7. the attorney general
8. secretary of the interior
9. secretary of agriculture
10. secretary of commerce
11. secretary of labor
12. secretary of health and human services

And If the President Is Disabled . . .

The vice president acts as president but does not assume the job itself.

The president can declare himself disabled and request that the vice president assume his duties. Additionally, the president can be declared disabled (should the president be unconscious, for instance) by a majority vote of the vice president and the members of the president's cabinet. In either case, it is the president's right to determine when he is able to assume the powers and duties of the office again.

If the vice president and members of the cabinet disagree with the president's assessment of his own fitness, they can request that both Houses of Congress put the matter to a vote. A two-thirds vote is required by both Houses to overrule the president's wish to return to power.

Actually, General Haig, You've Got It Wrong. The President's Still in Charge.

"I hope you're all Republicans."
—Reagan's quip to the surgeons who were about to operate on him after he was shot

It's worth mentioning that Reagan kept a much cooler head after being shot than did his secretary of state Alexander Haig—while the general was putting his foot in his mouth, the wounded president was entertaining the troops with a string of one-liners.

"Honey, I forgot to duck!" was the first thing Reagan said to his wife, Nancy, after he was shot. What an actor! Is it possible he remembered, even under those circumstances, that this was the same thing boxer Jack Dempsey had said to his wife fifty-five years earlier after he was pulverized in the ring by Gene Tunney?

PRESIDENT . . . FOR A DAY

Only once has the country been under the leadership of someone other than the president or vice president.

Sort of.

It happened on March 4, 1849, when Inauguration Day fell on a Sunday and president-elect Zachary Taylor refused to be inaugurated on the Sabbath. This created a bit of a stir because, even though he refused to take his vow of office that day, the law still said that on March 4 at noon the current president and vice president would cease to be in power.

What to do? Well, according to the laws at the time, and if the position of vice president were ever vacant, it would be filled immediately by the president pro tem of the Senate. (If the position of president were ever vacant, it would be filled immediately by the vice president.) For all the reasons stated above, at noon on Sunday, March 4, 1849, the current president, James Polk, and his vice president, George Dallas, completed their terms in office and David Rice Atchinson, president pro tem of the Senate, became vice president. And at twelve o'clock on the same day, acting Vice President David Rice Atchinson also stepped in to become president of the United States.

"Nope. You're Not Invited."

Every year, when the president delivers his State of the Union address, there is one member of his cabinet who is not invited.

Think about it: The president's got to be there, obviously. And the vice president's got to be there to show his support for his boss. And the prez, of course, wants the rest of his cabinet there to cheer him on. . . .

But what if something happened? A devastating earthquake or a terrorist attack or a bomb? What if everyone in the room were killed? Who would lead the nation?

By law, therefore, at least one member of the president's cabinet is required to stay away on the night of the State of the Union address in case such a disaster occurs.

How to Beat an Assassin at His Own Game

It wasn't until 1901, when William McKinley was assassinated, that the president began receiving protection. Yet the first president to have an attempt made on his life was Andrew Jackson.

His would-be assassin was Richard Lawrence, a house painter who thought the president was the only thing standing between him and the British throne. Lawrence actually shot at the president twice, using two different guns.

But go figure the odds of this: Both guns misfired—an event that statisticians say could only occur once in 125,000 tries.

Once Jackson got over the shock of being shot at, he chased after Lawrence with his walking stick.

"Quick! Call a Lawyer!"
President Dies of Malpractice

James Garfield didn't die from gunshot wounds—he died of blood poisoning after doctors tried to fish a bullet out of his back with their dirty fingers and instruments. (Poor guy. He took the bullet in the back before doctors had a clue about infections . . . so they didn't even bother washing their hands before they started poking around in his wound.)

If Garfield showed up at an emergency room today with the same wounds, the doctors in attendance probably would have left the bullet right where it was. And then they would have sent him home after a few days of observation and bed rest—instead of causing him to linger on in pain for eighty days before dying.

In fact, during his trial Garfield's assassin, Charles Guiteau, claimed he wasn't the one that killed the president; that job, he claimed, had been done by his doctors.

> **"Go out and buy every pound of ice you can find!
> Hurry! This stifling air is killing the president!"**
> —FIRST LADY LUCRETIA GARFIELD

Unbeknownst to most, the shooting of President Garfield provided the catalyst for the invention of the first air conditioner.

First, he was surrounded by blocks of ice while his wife and staffers waved fans to blow the cooler air over his body—but this had only the slightest impact on the heat.

Next, an inventor named R. S. Jennings and a group of military engineers tried to build a cooling system using ice water and an electric fan—which brought the temperature of the room down but made it so humid it was almost impossible to breath.

Finally, after seventy-two hours of nonstop work, a system was developed that pumped cool air from three tons of ice into the president's room while the moisture from the melting ice was channeled away in a series of Rube Goldberg-like tubes and ducts.

Air conditioning was born. But eighty days after he was shot, the president died. When it comes to the medical sciences, it's amazing what a difference thirty years makes:

- Garfield was shot in 1881.
- Doctors tried to remove Garfield's bullet.

- Garfield died eighty days after he was shot.

- Teddy Roosevelt was shot in 1912.
- Doctors left Roosevelt's bullet right where it landed.

- Roosevelt lived for seven more years.

And to Add Insult to Injury

If his doctors had found the bullet,
President Garfield might have had a good
chance of living. However, since the doctors
couldn't find it they just kept poking around
with their dirty hands and medical tools,
thus making matters worse.
Interestingly, one method they used to try to
find the bullet involved a brand-new invention by
Alexander Graham Bell: a metal detector.
And it might have helped too—if Garfield
hadn't been lying on a metal bed!

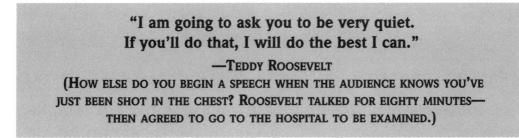

"I am going to ask you to be very quiet.
If you'll do that, I will do the best I can."

—TEDDY ROOSEVELT

(HOW ELSE DO YOU BEGIN A SPEECH WHEN THE AUDIENCE KNOWS YOU'VE
JUST BEEN SHOT IN THE CHEST? ROOSEVELT TALKED FOR EIGHTY MINUTES—
THEN AGREED TO GO TO THE HOSPITAL TO BE EXAMINED.)

During Teddy Roosevelt's second run for the presidency he became the first former president to survive an assassination attempt.

He was shot while in Milwaukee to deliver a speech, yet still delivered the speech with the bullet in his chest. Afterward he was rushed to a hospital, where it was discovered that the bullet had nicked his glasses case, slowing its impact. Additionally, Roosevelt had written his speech by hand on single pieces of paper in large letters with wide spaces for easy reading, so the fifty-page speech (which he had folded in half and put in his left breast pocket) helped slow the speed of the bullet.

"No doubt about it," commented Roosevelt's doctor, Alexander Lamber. "His speech saved his life."

"I don't mind it any more than
if it were in my waistcoat pocket."

—TR, MAKING AN OBSERVATION ABOUT THE BULLET
IN HIS CHEST MANY YEARS AFTER HE WAS SHOT

Dead Dumb

On July 4, 1850, in the fourth year of his presidency, Zachary Taylor attended a ceremony for the laying of the cornerstone of the Washington Monument. While at the reception he ate a huge amount of cold cherries and pickled cucumbers and drank a massive quantity of iced milk.
Five days later he was dead of gastroenteritis.

★ ★ ★

James Polk worked so hard at being president that he may have worked himself to death. For the full four years of his presidency he worked twelve to fourteen hours a day; he hated to stop working even to eat. Three months after he left office he was dead of exhaustion.

DEAD DOG

Warren Harding loved dogs.

In fact, he loved his own dog, Laddie Boy, so much that he arranged for him to be assigned Dog License #1 and threw him a birthday party at the White House, where he was served a cake made of layered dog biscuits covered with frosting.

Another time, Harding heard about a dog that had been brought into the country illegally and was going to be put to death by the order of a Pennsylvania judge. Harding was so moved by the story he wrote a letter to the governor of Pennsylvania requesting a pardon for the dog . . . which the governor granted.

When the newspaperman-turned-politician died, the Newsboys Association of America, of which Harding was also president, decided to build a statue of Laddie Boy as a tribute to him. To raise money for the statue, the newsboys association asked each

---

Finally . . . the answer is here!

★ ★ ★

Q: Who is buried in Grant's Tomb?

A: No one. No one is ever buried in a tomb—tombs are always above ground.

newspaper boy in America to donate a penny. One hundred and three pounds of pennies were collected and then melted down to provide the bronze for the statue.

The statue of Laddie Boy can still be seen today at the Smithsonian Institute.

DEATH DEFYING

Health. Fitness. It's a national craze.

Here are a few odd things presidents have done to maintain their health, ward off illness, or otherwise tempt the hands of fate:

- Ronald and Nancy Reagan gave up smoking after their good friend Robert Taylor died of lung cancer. As the story goes, Reagan needed something to help him kick the habit, and his love of jellybeans was born.
- Thomas Jefferson was convinced that if he soaked his feet in a bucket of cold water every day he'd never get a cold.
- Sure to cure what ails ya': Calvin Coolidge used to like having his head rubbed with petroleum jelly while he ate his breakfast in bed.
- After Woodrow Wilson's first wife died, his doctor encouraged him to take up the game of golf to help him relax and get over her death. Wilson fell in love with the game and was soon playing every day before breakfast. He liked playing so much, in fact, that in winter he would paint his golf balls black so he could continue playing in the snow.

- Jimmy Carter had problems with his stomach and feet that made him think he'd never get into the navy. To cure his flat feet he would stand around on Coke bottles (being from Georgia, Pepsi just wouldn't do) and roll them back and forth under his feet. The problem with his stomach was even more easily solved: He carried a bucket around the ship with him when it was his turn to stand watch.
- Ulysses S. Grant had a pack-a-day habit—only it wasn't twenty cigarettes he smoked every day, it was twenty cigars.
- No one liked a good toothpick more than Warren G. Harding. In fact, he had the White House staff stash them all around the house so he would never have to travel far to get one.

> "Since I came to the White House, I got two hearing aids, a colon operation, skin cancer, a prostate operation, and I was shot. The damn thing is I've never felt better in my life."
> —RONALD REAGAN IN 1987

"PSSSSSST! CATO, IS THAT YOU?"

Much like Inspector Clouseau of the Pink Panther movies, Teddy Roosevelt lived for his violent and relentless daily exercise. He fought with Japanese jujitsu experts and Chinese wrestlers in the East Room. He walked hard, running his friends down and challenging the Secret Service men who were there to protect him to keep up as he crossed rivers and streams, climbed up and down hills, and cut through the underbrush. He played tennis and rode horseback daily. He was also the first president to jog; he ran around the Washington Monument every day.

Once, while boxing with a young naval officer, he took a blow to the left eye that eventually caused him to lose the use of it (although Teddy kept this a secret for many years so the naval officer wouldn't feel guilty).

> **"I do little boxing now because it seems rather absurd for a president to appear with a black eye or a swollen nose or a cut lip."**
> —TEDDY ROOSEVELT

THIS KIND OF TALK CAN KILL YOU

*T*he record for both the longest inauguration speech and the shortest presidency both belong to one man: William Henry Harrison. Harrison died after only thirty-one days in office, and it's fair to say that he talked himself into his grave.

Here's the longer version of the story:

Harrison's inauguration was on a cold and wet day, yet Harrison refused to wear a hat, coat, or gloves and insisted on participating in all of the outdoor events. This included the presentation of his inauguration speech, which was 8,578 words long and lasted one hour and forty-five minutes.

One month later Harrison was dead from pneumonia.

"Excuse me? Did you say something?"

★ ★ ★

It was George Washington who made the shortest inauguration speech on record—133 words and less than two minutes long.

MODEST TO THE END

Before he died Thomas Jefferson wrote his own epitaph:

Here was buried Thomas Jefferson, author of the Declaration of Independence, of the Statuette of Virginia for Religious Freedom, and the father of the University of Virginia.

You'll notice Jefferson neglected to mention he had ever been the president of the United States.

CURSES!

When William Henry Harrison was a young man fighting at the Battle of Tippercanoe, a Shawnee Indian put a curse on his head. As a result, they say, Harrison died a month after he took office. And until 1980 all other presidents elected in a year ending in zero also died while in office—Lincoln, McKinley, Harding, Kennedy.

MORE CURSES!

Call it character assassination if you want. Or call it death of a career.

When the leader of Haiti, Jean Claude Duvalier, came to the conclusion that Jimmy Carter was treating him and his countrymen badly, he did the only logical thing: He headed for the backyard at midnight on a dark Haitian night and put a curse on the president's head by chanting and throwing a live bull, some photos of Carter, and a lot of dirt into a very large hole.

Did it work? You be the judge. Shortly after Duvalier cast his midnight spell:

- Fifty-two American hostages were taken in Iran during an election year and Carter couldn't get them out.
- Inflation soared out of control, and prime interest rates reached as high as 20 percent.
- Carter's popularity plunged.
- Carter lost the 1980 election to Ronald Reagan.

DEATH WISH

- According to family history, George Washington insisted he be embalmed in whiskey for three days after his death, just to be sure he was really gone before they buried him.
- Andrew Jackson, who came within one Senate vote of being impeached, requested he be buried with a copy of the Constitution under his head as a pillow and the Stars and Stripes wrapped over him like a shroud.
- One might have thought "Silent Cal" Coolidge would use his will as the instrument to finally speak his mind, but he didn't. Instead he left this world in the same spirit in which he had lived—practically silent. Coolidge's entire will, in which he left everything he owned to his wife and made it quite explicit he was leaving nothing to his one surviving son, consisted of one sentence.
- JFK, who was independently wealthy and a member of one of the richest and most powerful families in the country, left his wife all of his "personal effects, furniture, furnishings, silverware, dishes, china, glassware, and linens, which I may own at the time of death" along with a grand total of twenty-five thousand dollars in cash.
- When Andrew Johnson died his family wanted to "do the right thing" and throw him a proper funeral. But before Johnson died he had expressly forbade them to call in a minister to do the job.

> **"Please put out the light."**
> —TEDDY ROOSEVELT'S LAST REQUEST BEFORE DYING

DEAD LAST

*E*ver wonder just how far you could take a rivalry?

While John Adams lay dying on July 4, 1826—exactly fifty years to the day after the Declaration of Independence was signed—he resigned himself to the fact that his most bitter political rival, Thomas Jefferson, would live on and beat him again.

Thus Adams's last words were, "Thomas Jefferson survives."

Little did Adams know that Jefferson had died just a few hours earlier.

> **"This is the fourth?"**
> —THOMAS JEFFERSON'S LAST WORDS.
> THE FIRST TIME HE ASKED, IT WAS STILL JULY 3.

8

GOOFBALLS!

WELL, MAYBE IF PEOPLE TIPTOED around you all the time and were always calling you "the most powerful man in the world," you might start to believe it too. And all that power might start to affect your behavior in some pretty strange ways.

On the other hand, if you're like us, you've probably already done some pretty strange things, never once imagining that every small utterance and tiny goofy act you ever committed would someday be scrutinized by voters, journalists, historians, and nosy busybodies like you and us.

Such is the lot of the president: Every moment of his life is under a microscope, even those years before he even entertained the notion that he would someday become president.

GOOFBALL-AT-A-GLANCE

Or maybe he couldn't find an ATM.

PRESIDENT: George Washington

RANDOM GOOFY ACT(S): Washington didn't have enough money to get to his own inauguration, so he had to borrow six hundred dollars from a neighbor.

PRESIDENT: John Adams

RANDOM GOOFY ACT(S):
- While he was serving as the U.S. minister to England and Thomas Jefferson was serving as the U.S. minister to France, the two men made a trip to Stratford-upon-Avon to visit the birthplace of William Shakespeare. While there, the two men took a knife to one of Shakespeare's chairs so they could take home some woodchips as souvenirs.
- He and his wife once got lost in the woods of Washington, D.C., on their way to the White House. They might still be there if a passing stranger hadn't shown them the way home.

Goofballs!

PRESIDENT: **Thomas Jefferson**

RANDOM GOOFY ACT(S):
- He had the honor of leading the first inaugural parade through Washington. However, a parade wasn't exactly what he had in mind—he was just walking back to his boarding house after being sworn in, and a bunch of people decided to follow.
- When the British minister to the United States arrived at the White House for his first meeting with the new president, Jefferson received him wearing only his robe and his slippers.

PRESIDENT: **James Madison**

RANDOM GOOFY ACT(S): He and Thomas Jefferson were once arrested together for taking a carriage ride in the countryside of Vermont on a Sunday, which violated the blue laws of that state.

PRESIDENT: **James Monroe**

RANDOM GOOFY ACT(S): Poor James Monroe. . . . When it was time for him to be inaugurated, he couldn't have his ceremony in the chamber of the House of Representatives as all his predecessors had done. The problem? He and Speaker of the House Henry Clay were having a tiff, so Clay put his foot down and refused to let Monroe use the hall.

America's first cover-up in the press!

PRESIDENT: **John Quincy Adams**

RANDOM GOOFY ACT(S): While president, he would often go from the White House to the edge of the Potomac River, shuck off his clothes, throw them on a rock, and go skinny-dipping. One day, when he returned to the rock, he found a reporter sitting on his mound of clothes. And it wasn't just any reporter. It was a woman named Anne Royal. And she refused to leave until the president granted her an interview. Adams was only too happy to oblige her request—without getting out of the river, of course.

There is an additional irony to this story: There was Royal sitting his clothes, yet when John Quincy was back at the White House he did not like "regular" people to sit in his presence, so he would make sure there weren't enough chairs to go around.

PRESIDENT: **Andrew Jackson**

RANDOM GOOFY ACT(S): • One of the first things he did after being elected president was to order twenty spittoons for the White House parlors.
• He was the first president to be handed a baby to kiss as a part of his campaigning duties—but he declined the offer and passed the baby to his secretary of war instead.
• When he sent his first annual message to Congress in 1829, it was so well received that no one could believe he wrote it. When he was accused point-blank of having sent in a message

written by someone else, he replied, "Don't I deserve just as much credit for picking out the man who could write it?"

• While president, he kept a stable of thoroughbreds on the White House grounds. But when he entered them into races at a nearby track, he used an alias so no one would know they were his.

Can you guess what came between him and his Calvin Kleins?

PRESIDENT: Martin Van Buren

RANDOM GOOFY ACT(S): Rumor has it he was quite a dandy and used to dab a little cologne on his whiskers and lace himself up in a corset every day.

PRESIDENT: William Henry Harrison

RANDOM GOOFY ACT(S):
• His campaign slogan during the 1840 presidential campaign was "Keep the Ball Rolling to Washington." Of course his supporters had no choice but to roll a huge ball of paper across the country to the Whig convention in Baltimore.
• He was sometimes called "General Mum" because he never spoke out on any of the major issues while campaigning for president. This was no accident; the truth was that he had nothing to say.

"Wunnerful! Wunnerful!"

PRESIDENT: John Tyler

RANDOM GOOFY ACT(S): He loved to dance. In fact, he's the guy who made the polka an American household word.

PRESIDENT: James Polk

RANDOM GOOFY ACT(S):
- At age sixteen he had an operation to have his gallstones removed . . . and demanded the operation be done without anesthesia.
- A matter of great concern to him as president was how to protect his arm from injury after a day of handshaking . . . and he was sure he'd found the trick:

  I could shake hands during the whole day without suffering any bad effects from it. . . . If a man surrendered his arm to be shaken, by some horizontally, by others perpendicularly, and by others again with a strong grip, he could not fail to suffer severely from it, but that if he would shake and not be shaken, grip and not be gripped, taking care always to squeeze the hand of his adversary as hard as he squeezed him, that he suffered no inconvenience from it. . . . I could generally anticipate when I was to have a strong grip, and that when I observed a strong man approaching I generally took advantage of him by being a little quicker then he was and seizing him by the tips of his fingers, giving him a hearty shake, and thus preventing him from getting a full grip upon me.

Maybe Polk Wasn't So Goofy After All

In the good old days when security was less of a problem and there were events at the White House that were open to the public, presidents would sometimes shake as many as eight thousand hands at a stretch, at the rate of forty to fifty per minute. On one particular occasion, after Abe Lincoln had spent a full three hours at a reception pressing the flesh before signing an important bill, he found his arm was "almost paralyzed" and it was next to impossible for him to hold onto a pen. After dropping his writing instrument once, he persevered and picked it up again . . . to sign the Emancipation Proclamation into law.

PRESIDENT: Zachary Taylor

RANDOM GOOFY ACT(S): He had no political experience when nominated for president, had never voted before, and didn't even know what party he belonged to. When the notification of his nomination for president arrived in the mail he didn't respond to it—not because he didn't want the job but because he was too cheap to pay the ten cents of postage due.

PRESIDENT: Millard Fillmore

RANDOM GOOFY ACT(S): One of his greatest accomplishments as president? He successfully negotiated a treaty with Peru for the use of bird droppings.

Another of Fillmore's great accomplishments? He bought the White House's first stove. When the cook couldn't figure out how to use it, Fillmore went down to the Patent Office, studied the drawings until he understood how it worked, then went back to the White House and taught the cook.

Goofballs!

PRESIDENT: Franklin Pierce

RANDOM GOOFY ACT(S): *Ben, they tell me you are going to vote for the abolition resolutions. Now, I am not here, of course, to dictate to you; but if you vote for those resolutions . . . you are no brother of mine; I will never speak to you again.*

Just Like Motel 6, Part One:
The highest-priced rooms of any national chain

PRESIDENT: James Buchanan

RANDOM GOOFY ACT(S): As rumors fly about President Clinton and the 938 close friends of his who have spent the night at the White House (otherwise known as Motel Sixteen Hundred) it is worthwhile to take pause and recall that James Buchanan was the first president to be visited by a member of the Royal Family. Buchanan considered the visit to be such an honor that he let Prince Albert Edward sleep in his bed while he slept on a couch out in the hall.

PRESIDENT: **Abraham Lincoln**

RANDOM GOOFY ACT(S):
- It was during a cabinet meeting at which all his cabinet members disagreed with him that he summed up his position this way: "Seven nays, one aye; the ayes have it."
- Once, before he was president, he led twenty or so soldiers on a march during the Black Hawk Indian War. When they reached a fence with a gate, he couldn't for the life of him remember the proper marching order to give the men so they would proceed single file through the gate. So, after thinking for a minute, he ordered, "This company is dismissed for two minutes, when it will fall in again on the other side of the gate."
- He is the only president to have faced enemy fire while in office. It happened when he was visiting Fort Stevens during the Civil War; he mounted a parapet to get a better view of the battlefield, and being six feet four, he made an easy mark. Rumor has it that when a solider (said to be future Supreme Court Justice Oliver Wendell Holmes) shouted at him to "Get down, you damned fool, before you get shot!" the president did as he was told.
- No one loved puns and wordplay more than he did. When Stephen Douglas referred to him as "two-faced," he replied by asking, "If I had another face, do you think I would wear this one?" When he saw a heavyset woman in a large feathered cap fall down as she was crossing the street, he commented: "Reminds me of a duck. . . . She's got feathers on her head and down on her behind." And when he heard a rumor that Edward

Stanton, his secretary of war, had called him "a damned fool," he gave this honest reply: "If Stanton said I was a damned fool, then I must be one, for he is nearly always right and generally says what he means."

PRESIDENT: **Andrew Johnson**

RANDOM GOOFY ACT(S):
- Before he got into politics, he was a tailor—the only tailor ever to be elected president. Even as president it was rare for him to pass a tailor shop—no matter where he was—without stopping in to say hello. He was so proud of his skill with a needle and thread that while governor of Tennessee he took time out from his gubernatorial duties to make a suit for a friend, who just happened to be the governor of Kentucky. The grateful governor, previously a blacksmith, sent him a shovel and a pair of tongs in return.
- Even as president, he wore only suits that were tailor-made . . . by his own hand.

PRESIDENT: **Ulysses S. Grant**

RANDOM GOOFY ACT(S):
- As a boy, his father sent him to a neighbor's house to buy a colt for which his father had already offered twenty dollars but that the neighbor insisted was worth twenty-five. The last set of instructions his father gave him was to offer twenty, and if the

neighbor wouldn't take it, to offer twenty-two fifty. Only as a last resort was he to offer the full twenty-five. When he got to the neighbor's house he immediately reported: "Papa says I may offer you twenty dollars for the colt, but if you won't take that I am to offer twenty-two and a half, and if you won't take that, to give you twenty-five."

- He was actually given the name Hiram Ulysses Grant but hated the acronym his name created: HUG. Therefore, when his name was incorrectly recorded as Ulysses Simpson Grant while a student at West Point, he never bothered to point out the error.
- Although he was a great war hero, anytime he saw blood or a piece of raw meat his head would start to spin.
- He had a thing about nudity; he didn't like it. He refused to ever get completely naked—not even to bathe—and at the age of sixty claimed that no one had seen him without clothes since he was a little boy.
- While walking in the rain to a reception in his honor one day, he offered to share his umbrella with another man headed the same way. The man, it turned out, was also going to the reception and confided, "I merely go to satisfy a personal curiosity. Between us, I have always thought that Grant was very much an overrated man." "That's my view also," was Grant's reply.

Goofballs!

Just Like Motel 6, Part Two: "Children sleep for free!"

PRESIDENT: Rutherford B. Hayes

RANDOM GOOFY ACT(S): Like the Clintons, he and his family liked to entertain a lot of guests at the White House. Sometimes, when they invited too many people to spend the night, son Webb had to sleep on top of an old billiards table in the White House attic.

PRESIDENT: James Garfield

RANDOM GOOFY ACT(S): He was the first president to ever talk on a telephone. Here's what he said to Alexander Graham Bell, who was at the other end of a thirteen-mile wire, to mark this momentous occasion: "Please speak a little more slowly."

Bet Motel 6 wouldn't turn them away.

PRESIDENT: Chester Alan Arthur

RANDOM GOOFY ACT(S): He enacted the country's first major immigration law: His goal was to prevent criminals, paupers, idiots, and the insane from entering the country.

PRESIDENT: Grover Cleveland

RANDOM GOOFY ACT(S): He is the only president ever to get married in the White House. He wrote the invitations himself and worked in his office until 7 P.M. on the day of the wedding, then knocked off so he could get ready for the ceremony and reception. And while he did promise to "love, honor, and comfort" his bride, he refused to promise to "obey" her.

Just like Motel 6, Part Three: "We'll leave a light on for you."

PRESIDENT: Benjamin Harrison

RANDOM GOOFY ACT(S): He and his family were the first to have electricity in the White House—but they left the lights on all night because they were afraid to touch the switches.

PRESIDENT: William McKinley

RANDOM GOOFY ACT(S): He loved a good cigar but wouldn't be photographed with one in his mouth; he didn't want to set a bad example for America's children, after all.

Goofballs!

PRESIDENT: **Teddy Roosevelt**

RANDOM GOOFY ACT(S):
- While hunting one day, he came across a small bear cub and of course refused to shoot it. The incident was reported in the news, which inspired a political cartoonist to draw his interpretation of the scene, which then inspired a toy manufacturer to come out with a line of stuffed animals he called "Teddy Bears." Ironically, President Roosevelt hated to be called Teddy.
- Teddy Roosevelt . . . Madison Avenue copywriter? Well, it has been said that after drinking a cup of Maxwell House coffee while visiting Andrew Jackson's home, the Hermitage, near Nashville, Roosevelt said, "Delicious. This coffee is good to the last drop!"

PRESIDENT: **William Howard Taft**

RANDOM GOOFY ACT(S):
- While a young lawyer, he visited another town on business and discovered the next train home was many hours away. Taking a second look at the train schedule, he saw that a faster train would be passing soon, but wasn't scheduled to stop at his station. Without hesitation he sent a wire to the superintendent of the line asking if the train could stop at his station for a large party. Of course, when he climbed aboard the train alone, the conductor looked puzzled. Taft looked him in the eye, made a gesture toward his three-hundred-pound frame, and told the conductor he was the "large party" for which the train was making the special stop.

193

- When you're as heavy as Taft was, people will nag you to death trying to get you to lose weight. This is true even if you are president, as he found out; between his wife and his doctor, he was often on a diet, and whenever he was dieting he would get cranky. Once, when he went off on a train trip, he became enraged at discovering his wife had had the dining car removed. "What's the use of being president if you can't have a train with a diner on it?" he asked and demanded that the crew stop at the next station and restore the dining car to its rightful place.

- Perhaps it was because of his size, but he sometimes had a heck of a time staying awake. His aide, Archie Butts, had one method of waking him when others were around: He would cough. His wife employed a slightly different technique: She'd give him an elbow in the ribs.

PRESIDENT: **Woodrow Wilson**

RANDOM GOOFY ACT(S): He was the first president to earn a Ph.D., but in his heart he wanted to be a vaudeville actor. As a young boy, he even ran away to join the circus—and went home with padding in his pants in anticipation of the greeting he was going to get from his father.

PRESIDENT: **Warren Harding**

RANDOM GOOFY ACT(S): See the *Goofball Hall of Fame* on page 205.

PRESIDENT: **Calvin Coolidge**

RANDOM GOOFY ACT(S): See the *Goofball Hall of Fame* on page 205.

Just like Motel 6, Part Four: "Friendly Service!"

PRESIDENT: **Herbert Hoover**

RANDOM GOOFY ACT(S): Under his reign the White House servants quickly learned one thing: The president didn't like to see them. According to one account:

> *[Hoover] did not like seeing the servants in the halls; and so they hid when the White House bells announced his presence, footmen holding trays high in the air as they scurried into hall closets already crowded with maids.*

PRESIDENT: **Franklin Delano Roosevelt**

RANDOM GOOFY ACT(S): • He was a rich, good-looking guy who just happened to have a cousin in the White House. No surprise, then, that his own local politicians began to court him and encourage him to enter local politics. One story has it that when he was first approached by a local political boss and encouraged to enter the race for the

New York state assembly, his first response was that he would consider it, but he wanted to talk to his mother about it first. "Frank," the local politician replied, "there are men back in Poughkeepsie waiting for your answer. They won't like to hear that you had to ask your mother."

- When visited at the White House by the king and queen of England, he let Eleanor serve them hot dogs for dinner.
- His idea of a good time was to play poker with lots of wild cards. He also loved collecting stamps and never left on a trip without taking at least one of his stamp albums with him.
- He had "Stolen from the White House" embossed on the White House matches.

PRESIDENT: **Harry Truman**

RANDOM GOOFY ACT(S):
- He loved to use the word *manure*. Once asked why she let him use such language, his wife, Bess, explained that it took her twenty years to get him to say just that.
- In his early days of politics he joined the Ku Klux Klan in Jackson County, Missouri, because he knew he couldn't win the judge's seat he was running for without their support; a year after he was elected he resigned his membership and got his ten-dollar membership fee back.

- When he visited Disneyland he refused to ride on the "Dumbo, the Elephant" ride because he was a Democrat and the elephant, of course, is the mascot of the Republican Party.

"General Picasso, Sir!"

PRESIDENT: **Dwight D. Eisenhower**

RANDOM GOOFY ACT(S): He loved to paint but couldn't draw worth a darn, so he would have someone else sketch pictures, and then he would paint inside the lines. Believe it or not, this is how the national paint-by-numbers fad of the 1950s began.

PRESIDENT: **John F. Kennedy**

RANDOM GOOFY ACT(S): • As a young man, he seemed to have a good mind for his studies but was clueless about the world. As he once described himself: "Though I may not be able to remember material things such as tickets, gloves, and so on I can remember things like Ivanhoe, and the last time we had an exam on it I got ninety-eight." At the age of thirteen in 1930, while the rest of the country was suffering from the debilitating effects of the stock market crash and the Great Depression, Jack wrote home: "Please send me the *Literary Digest* because I didn't know about the Market Slump until a long time after."

- He had a hard time with the concept of money for all of his adult life. For one thing, he never seemed to have any cash on him—which meant his friends were constantly shelling out money to cover the costs of his cabs and dinners and movies. Perhaps it was really his father's fault; even though Joe Sr. was one of the richest men in the country and was at one time head of the Securities and Exchange Commission, he forbade any of his children to talk about money at the dinner table.
- When he appointed his brother Robert to the position of attorney general, he jokingly remarked that he wanted to see his little brother get some legal experience as a government lawyer before he had to go out into the real world and try his hands at private practice.

PRESIDENT: **Lyndon B. Johnson**

RANDOM GOOFY ACT(S):
- He won his first seat in the Senate by campaigning all over Texas in a helicopter. Every time he spotted someone (or a town or city) down below he'd boom out over the copter's PA: "Hello down there. This is your friend, Lyndon Johnson."
- As part of his drive to prove to the American people that the government could spend their money wisely, he would turn off every light in the White House he felt was burning unnecessarily. Unfortunately for everyone else, this meant that if they left

their offices for even a few minutes they were likely to return to a dark room—not to mention a walk down a dark White House hallway bumping into other staff members and aides.
- He often called spontaneous press conferences and had surprised journalists walk along with him as he gave them a briefing. The only problem was that he walked so fast everyone had to run to keep up with him—which made it hard to listen carefully, ask intelligent questions, or carry on a conversation. But he was a great fan of these fast-paced press conferences, which he called "Walkie-Talkies."

PRESIDENT: **Richard Nixon**

RANDOM GOOFY ACT(S):
- According to a former Secret Service agent, when Nixon went to the doctor he liked to put the hospital gown on backward and "tramp down the hall with the front flying open. The nurses would stop in their tracks."
- Once, just before doing an interview with David Frost, he turned to Frost and asked: "Well, did you do any fornicating this weekend?"
- While speaking at a Junior Chamber of Commerce meeting, he reflected on a trip he once made to Caracas, Venezuela, where he had been pelted by stones: "I got stoned in Caracas," he said. "I'll tell you one thing; it's a lot different from getting stoned at a Jaycee convention."

PRESIDENT: Gerald Ford

RANDOM GOOFY ACT(S):
- Rumor has it he showed up for his wedding with a brown shoe on one foot and a black shoe on the other.
- One night when he took his dog out for a walk, he discovered he had locked himself out of the White House. Just as he resigned himself to the fact he was going to have to spend the night outside in his robe and slippers, a guard discovered him and let him back in.
- His wife, Betty, once woke up and heard him talking in his sleep: "Thank you, thank you, thank you, thank, you, thank you," he said over and over again. When she woke him, he told her he had again been dreaming of standing in a receiving line.

PRESIDENT: Jimmy Carter

RANDOM GOOFY ACT(S):
- When he was a boy, he took his mother's diamond engagement ring to school and gave it to his teacher, Mrs. Forrest, with this explanation: "My daddy can always buy Momma another one."
- Fifty-four years after FDR's first "Fireside Chat," he tried to duplicate FDR's success, appearing on television in the Oval Office beside a roaring fire, wearing a cardigan sweater instead of the traditional presidential suit. While his fireside chat may not have gone over as well as FDR's did, it did earn him a new nickname: "Jimmy Cardigan." He also tried his hand at communicating with the people via a call-in TV talk show called *Ask Mr.*

Carter. For two hours he took calls from the American people. A total of nine million people called to ask a question of the president; only forty-two callers actually got through.

PRESIDENT: **Ronald Reagan**

RANDOM GOOFY ACT(S):
- He was named West Coast Father of the Year in 1976—the same year he forbade daughter Patti from bringing her boyfriend home because the two were living in sin.
- As a sportscaster for WHO in Des Moines, he would fake the play-by-play of Chicago Cubs games by making up the plays as he read a news ticker tape. One day the ticker tape died mid-game, so he had to improvise. For six minutes he had the batter swing at pitch after pitch and sent each hit over the foul line until the ticker tape began to run again and he could return to reporting on the actual game.

PRESIDENT: **George Bush**

RANDOM GOOFY ACT(S): According to the book *Marching In Place, The Status Quo Presidency of George Bush* by *Time* magazine White House correspondents Michael Duffy and Dan Goodgame, George Bush elevated goofballness to an art form:

- While running for president in 1988, he spent Halloween night running through his campaign airplane wearing a rubber George Bush mask and shouting "Read my lips! Read my lips!"
- He once invited Saturday Night Live's Dana Carvey to the White House so the comedian who had become famous impersonating him could do his impersonation to his face. Soon, both Bush and Carvey were "doing Bush" at one another. And when, as Duffy and Goodgame say, Carvey began "chopping the air with one hand and talking about 'Daaaan Quaaaaayle—getting stronger, learning ev-er-y daaay,' Bush doubled over in laughter. . . . By the end of 1991 Bush was doing imitations-of-Carvey-doing-imitations-of-Bush during televised press conferences."
- Playing games and having a good time was a great Bush pastime. One of his favorite games as president was called "Light 'em up." Say Duffy and Goodgame:

After taking the oath of office, Bush resembled nothing so much as a medieval boy king who woke up one morning, found himself atop the throne, and began tugging at the bell ropes for servants, ordering up royal carriages, and scheduling banquets and tournaments. . . . A delighted Bush singlehandedly organized an all-White House horseshoe pitching contest, drawing up some of the ladders himself. . . . Bush's ebullience seemed limitless—as hundreds of local congressmen and political officials who attempted to buttonhole him during a presidential visit to their states would discover. Most solons try to put to good use the brief ride from the local airport into town, making a pitch for help with a local project or a hand in solving a snarled political problem. Bush, however, often preempted such appeals with an adult car game called "Light 'em up." In the back of his armored Cadillac limousine, Bush faced forward with his guest on the jump seat facing aft. As the limo moved through the streets, Bush would pick out someone from the crowd, usually an attractive woman or child, point, and wait until—pow!—eye contact and the victim realizes, He's looking at me! That's when the target "lit up." Because the limo was moving forward, it fell to the guest facing aft to report to the president when he asked, "Did I get her? Did I light her up?" And then the game would begin again.

He didn't inhale . . . and he didn't swallow either.

PRESIDENT:	**Bill Clinton**
RANDOM GOOFY ACT(S):	• In 1996 scientists came to the conclusion that chocolate can affect the same part of the brain that is turned on by smoking pot. When Clinton was asked to comment he explained that he had once tried some chocolate . . . but didn't swallow.
	• In February of 1994, Clinton visited a truck plant in Louisiana. In the course of his visit he spoke to the workers of the plant and in his remarks he recounted that his first vehicle had been a truck. But he didn't leave it at that. Instead, as the *New York Times* tells it, "Mr. Clinton confided that he had lined the truck

bed with Astroturf, adding with a sly grin, 'You don't want to know why.'"

Well, of course we all wanted to know why—but the next day the only explanation Clinton could give (other than the obvious one) was that he'd covered the truck bed with Astroturf so he could haul luggage in it. "It wasn't for what everybody thought it was for when I made the comment, I'll tell you that. I'm guilty of a lot of things, but I didn't ever do that."

- While Clinton was running his first presidential campaign in 1991, he was once asked the simple questions, "Do you watch much TV as you campaign across the country, and if so, what do you watch?" Here's what the president some call "Slick Willie" had to say:

  I'm not a big television watcher because I don't have much time to do it. So I do spend a lot of time doing it but normally I watch news programs and sports programs, and sometimes I come in very late at night and I'm all keyed up and I don't go to sleep, so I watch movies. . . . Sometimes I'll see Sixty Minutes *or* 20/20, *but I'm usually away. As a matter of fact, my staff, when I'm on the road, will tape the early network news so I can watch it when I get home. . . . I watch CNN a lot.*

As you can see, President Clinton is not a big television watcher because he doesn't have much time to do it. So he spends a lot of time doing it, as you can see.

GOOFBALL HALL OF FAME

Historians love to rate and rank our presidents. And when it comes to assessing which were the most successful and which were the biggest failures, their conclusions are pretty predictable.

- Nominees for Best President are consistently Washington, Jefferson, Lincoln, Roosevelt, and Roosevelt.
- Nominees for Worst President are consistently Harding, Harding, Harding, Buchanan, and Grant.

Of course, when perusing these ratings it is always important to consider the source. And the criteria.

For instance, we happen to think George Washington was a horrible president. And if you thumb back through this book you'll see why: He was a boring old fart who made absolutely no effort toward providing the media with gist for their headline mills. No affairs, no scandals, no corruption—he didn't even drink too much or fight with his wife. How much fun was that for the American public?

And we're not the only one who says so. Nathaniel Hawthorne came to the same conclusion, wondering if "anyone has ever seen Washington in the nude. . . . It is inconceivable. He had no nakedness, but was born with his clothes on, and his hair powdered, and made a stately bow on his first appearance in the world." And Emerson concurred: "Every hero becomes a bore at last. . . . They cry up the virtues of George Washington—Damn George Washington!"

Washington—historians can have him.

"And the Winner Is . . ."

Harding, on the other hand, is our kind of guy. His life was a mess. He had two mistresses, an illegitimate child, a handful of friends in appointed positions who were robbing the country blind, and he was totally unfit for the job. (And he was the first to admit it.) And to cap it all off, his vice president, Calvin Coolidge, was every bit the goofball he was.

Warren Harding just wanted to have fun. So he got himself elected president because, hey!, who has more toys and time and fun than the leader of the entire Western world?

Finally, Warren Harding's our kind of guy because he broke all the rules (objective, moral, constitutional, biblical, etc.), had a great time doing it, yet did such a great job of manipulating the nation and the press that the people were convinced he was a patriot, a great leader—hell, almost a saint—when he died.

The More Things Change . . .

★ ★ ★

Well, the *New York Times* certainly showed the world what it thought of Warren G. Harding at the time of his nomination:

> "The firm and perfect flower of the cowardice and imbecility of the senatorial cabal."

The paper reversed its opinion four months later and proclaimed that he was "gradually assuming undisputed leadership."

Did I Mention . . .

As president, Harding ran up a debt with his stockbroker of about two hundred thousand dollars. And then he died.

★ ★ ★

One of Warren Harding's favorite activities as president was to visit the Gayety Burlesque, which provided him with a special box seat where he could see but couldn't be seen.

Harding on Harding

"I am not fit for this office and
should never have been here."

★ ★ ★

"Oftentimes, as I sit here, I don't
seem to grasp that I am president."

★ ★ ★

"Jud, you have a college education, haven't
you? I don't know what to do or where to turn
on this taxation matter. Somewhere there
must be a book that tells all about it, where
I could go to straighten it out in my mind.
But I don't know where the book is, and
maybe I couldn't read it if I found it!"

Takes One to Know One

★ ★ ★

Perhaps *lazy* is the wrong word. Harding actually kept quite a rigorous schedule:

- He played table tennis every morning.
- He played tennis every afternoon.
- He played golf two days a week.
- He played poker two nights a week.
- At noon every day he took time for a little constitutional, which also gave him an opportunity to shake hands with White House visitors.

VICE-GOOFBALL

What're the odds?

You take a guy like Warren Harding, goofball par excellence, and you've got to wonder where (or how) he could ever find a vice president goofy enough to complement his lying, cheating, lazy, goofball ways. But Harding did it again; he achieved the impossible.

His name was Calvin Coolidge.

In contrast to Warren Harding, Calvin Coolidge was an honest, hardworking family man who filled the role of president quite competently. He took office following Harding's death in 1923 and was reelected in 1924. In his five and a half years in office Coolidge reduced the national debt by about $2 billion. He reduced federal taxes three times and cleaned up Harding's fiscal messes by attacking the U.S. budget system and tinkering with it until it ran more smoothly.

Then, in 1928, while things were going

along nicely and Americans everywhere were fat and happy and prosperous and Calvin Coolidge was an extremely popular man and it was assumed he would be easily reelected to a second term, he made this announcement to the press and the nation in typical Calvin Coolidge style: "I do not choose to run for president in 1928."

And that was all he said.

Calvin Speaks!

His nickname was "Silent Cal." He was famous for saying . . . *nothing.*
An actual press conference with Calvin Coolidge:

"Have you any statement on the campaign?"
"No."
"Can you tell us something about the world situation?"
"No."
"Any information about Prohibition?"
"No . . . [And] remember—don't quote me."

- While Coolidge didn't think much of all the pomp and circumstance of Washington, he never turned down an invitation. Yet, once at a party or function he would talk as little as possible and leave by ten P.M. When asked why he attended all these functions that he so obviously disliked he replied, "Got to eat somewhere."
- While attending a dinner party a woman seated near him bet she could get him to say three words. "You lose" was his only reply.

- A presidential aide once recalled a summons to the Oval Office by Coolidge one day. After arriving, the aide spent thirty minutes there in the room with the president—yet Silent Cal didn't say a word. Finally, confused, the aide got up to leave. When he reached the door Coolidge said, "Thank you for coming. I wanted to think."
- His first cabinet meeting after Harding's death lasted only fifteen minutes.

> ## "How could they tell?"
> —DOROTHY PARKER ON THE DEATH
> OF CALVIN COOLIDGE

Calvin Coolidge—a Real Barrel of Fun

- Calvin Coolidge's definition of fun? Riding the mechanical bucking horse he kept in his bedroom at the White House. He rode it almost every day.
- On his first day in the White House, Cal got so bored he called the same friend on the phone five times. Sometimes, when boredom set in, he would hit all the buttons on his desk at one time just to see everyone come running to see what was wrong.
- When Cal moved into the White House he brought his own rocking chair; he liked to sit on the front porch and rock at night but quit after becoming annoyed with crowds of curious passersby.
- Coolidge loved to go fishing, but he made the Secret Service bait his hook.

A Real Wild Guy!

★ ★ ★

But don't start thinking of him as a daredevil; given a choice, Cal always preferred that his chauffeur stick to a nice safe speed of about 16 mph.

"Who You Callin' Cheap?!"

Cal was not only famous for being tight with a word; he was also famous for being tight with a buck.

- When he was in the mood for a good cigar, Cal would reach for his stash of Fonseca Corona Fines deLuxe, which he got for twenty-one dollars per hundred. But when he wanted to share a cigar with a good friend he had another stash of cigars . . . that cost him about three cents apiece.
- To save money, Coolidge tried to raise chickens at the White House. But for some reason, the chickens never tasted quite right. The mystery of the weird-tasting chickens was finally solved when someone pointed out that the chickens were penned right over the spot where Teddy Roosevelt had once grown mint.
- Cal liked to wander around the White

And a Tightwad Too!

★ ★ ★

Cal once drove a White House cook to quit because Cal didn't believe it would take six whole hams to feed sixty people at a state dinner.

House late at night—in his nightshirt. He often snuck into the kitchen and tried to figure out where all the White House leftovers had been stashed.

The Further Adventures of Calvin Coolidge

One day, an aide from the Library of Congress made a trip to the White House to arrange all the books in the library. As he sorted books Coolidge's dog kept nipping at his feet. Finally he got tired of shooing the dog away and did what anyone might do: He chucked a book at it. But he missed the dog, and the book bounced once and then hit something hard behind the curtain . . . and out stepped the president, who had been hiding.

"Warm day," Coolidge said and quickly left the room.

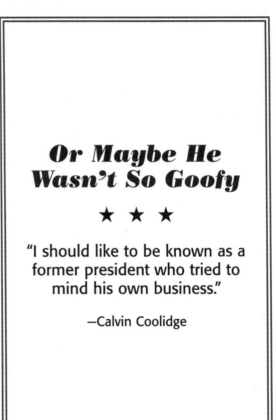

Or Maybe He Wasn't So Goofy

★ ★ ★

"I should like to be known as a former president who tried to mind his own business."

—Calvin Coolidge

9

VEEPS!

"Once upon a time there was a farmer
who had two sons. One of them ran
off to sea. The other was elected vice
president of the United States. Nothing
was ever heard of either of them again."

—THOMAS MARSHALL, VICE PRESIDENT UNDER WOODROW WILSON

* The word *Veep* was coined by the ten-year-old grandson of Vice President Alben Barkley.

*H*ERE'S WHY IT'S A ROTTEN JOB:

It's a ticket to public ridicule, powerlessness, and—for most—eventual oblivion. Of the forty-six vice presidents who have served, only fourteen have gone on to be president (and only five of those VPs got elected president; the rest moved up from the VP seat because of death or resignation and then either refused to run again or ran and lost). As VP Thomas Marshall implies above, the rest have been sent out to pasture and have never been heard from again.

Let's face it. The job of vice president was an afterthought on the part of the Constitutional Convention, put into the works for only one reason: so that if the president died or was otherwise unable to perform his duties, there would be someone there to replace him without the need for a special election.

> **"At a convintion nearly all th' dillygates lave as soon as they've nommyynated th' prisidint f'r fear wan iv thim will be mommyynated f'r vice presidint."**
>
> —A POLITICAL BOSS COMMENTING IN 1906 ON THE PROCESS OF CHOOSING A VICE PRESIDENT

The Veep isn't part of the legislative branch of the government. Nor is he a member of the executive branch. And if you read the Constitution literally, he is neither the president's subordinate nor someone to whom the president can, as a matter of course, give orders.

The vice president's only expressed responsibilities are:

- to preside over the Senate (But that doesn't mean he ever has to show up; most modern Veeps physically preside over the Senate less than 2 percent of the time it is in session.)
- to vote to break a tie (But he has no vote in the Senate at any other time.)

As for unexpressed duties:

- He serves on the boards of the National Security Council and the Board of Regents of the Smithsonian Institute.
- He names a total of five cadets to the three military academies, and he appoints senators to such commissions as the Migratory Bird Conservation Commission.

Anything else he does during his term is at the request of the president.

Jurassic Veeps?

★ ★ ★

Vice President Thomas Marshall once summed up his job as a regent of the Smithsonian Institute by describing it as "an opportunity [for the vice president] to compare his fossilized life with the fossils of all ages."

Much Ado about Not Much

★ ★ ★

Politics is power, and power can be summed up as the ability to spend and the ability to appoint. It should be noted then that in the 1880s the vice president had the power to make exactly four appointments: He could appoint his own secretary, his own private messenger, his own private telegraph operator, and—the appointment that was likely to be the most controversial—he had the power to appoint a restaurant-keeper for the Senate.

Suddenly, the glamour of it all washes away. Unlike the job of president (which is what all Veeps really want), the job of vice president begins to look like a dead end. But don't take my word for it. Let those who have served and those who have declined tell you in their own words.

"TELL HIM TO GO TO HELL"

—TRUMAN'S INITIAL RESPONSE WHEN HE HEARD FDR WANTED HIM TO RUN AS HIS VP

The room was crowded. Every damn political boss in the country was there, any of them you would want to name, and half a dozen governors.

And they all said, "Harry, we want you to be Vice President." I said, "I'm not going to do it."

Well, Bob Hannegan had put in a call to Roosevelt who was . . . down at San

Diego. They finally got him on the phone.
And with Roosevelt you didn't need a
phone. All you had to do was raise the
window and you could hear him.

I was sitting on one twin bed, and Bob
was on the other in this room, and
Roosevelt said [Mr. Truman gave a near-
perfect imitation of Roosevelt, Harvard
accent and all], Roosevelt said, "Bob, have
you got that guy lined up yet on that vice
Presidency?"

And Bob said, "No. He's the contrariest
goddamn mule from Missouri I ever saw."

"Well," Roosevelt said, "you tell him if
he wants to break up the Democratic
Party in the middle of the war and maybe
lose that war that's up to him."

—HARRY TRUMAN, IN THE BOOK
PLAIN SPEAKING, AN ORAL BIOGRAPHY
OF HARRY S TRUMAN

"Mind Your Manners!"

★ ★ ★

Even Harry's mom knew he was a
contrary mule. The first time Harry
phoned his mother after being
inaugurated as vice president, she
gave him these instructions:
"Now, you behave yourself up
there, Harry!"

> **"My country, in its wisdom, contrived for me the most insignificant office that ever the invention of man contrived or his imagination conceived."**
>
> —JOHN ADAMS, AMERICA'S FIRST VICE PRESIDENT

> **"Please accept my sincere sympathy."**
>
> —TELEGRAM FROM DEMOCRATIC VICE PRESIDENT MARSHALL TO NEWLY NOMINATED REPUBLICAN VP CANDIDATE CALVIN COOLIDGE

- Vice President Hannibal Hamlin understood the significance of his job. Therefore, at the beginning of each new Senate session, he would spend a few weeks presiding over that body and then request that the Senate choose a president pro tempore to stand in for him so he could go home to his farm in Maine and do something useful.

- Vice President Richard Johnson, too, understood his place in the scheme of things. For that reason he took a leave of absence from his job as Veep so he could open and then manage a hotel, tavern, resort, and spa on his property in Kentucky.

> **"As useful as a cow's fifth teat."**
>
> —HARRY TRUMAN ON THE VICE PRESIDENCY

> ## "A fifth wheel to a coach."
> —TEDDY ROOSEVELT ON THE VICE PRESIDENCY

- Vice President John Nance Garner was given virtually nothing to do by FDR, so he spent most of his time at his ranch in Uvalde, Texas, sitting on his porch shooting at a spittoon. Years later, when fellow Texan LBJ asked Garner if he should accept the vice presidential nomination, Garner replied: "The vice presidency ain't worth a pitcher of warm spit."

> "[Once, while visiting Denver] a big burley policeman kept following me around, until I asked him what he was doing. He said he was guarding my person. I said, 'Your labor is in vain. Nobody was ever crazy enough to shoot at a vice president. If you will go away and find somebody to shoot at me, I'll go down in history as being the first vice president who ever attracted enough attention even to have a crank shoot at him.'"
> —VICE PRESIDENT JOHN MARSHALL

- LBJ and his aides never dreamed that in 1960 he would be JFK's running mate . . . as the vice-presidential candidate. In fact, while Senator Kennedy crisscrossed the country stumping for the Democratic nomination, Johnson stayed in Washington; he was sure he'd get the nomination, and he felt his job as Senate majority leader required him to stay on the job.

    One of Johnson's aides was quoted as saying, "I can see it all now. Johnson will be standing in the hotel room after he wins the nomination, and he'll say, 'We want Sonny Boy for vice president. Go fetch him for me.'"

    When Kennedy won the nomination, Johnson explained his own loss this way: "Jack was out kissing babies while I was passing bills."

> ### "You die, I fly."
> —THEN VICE PRESIDENT GEORGE BUSH, MAKING THE
> SUCCINCT OBSERVATION THAT THE JOB OF VP CONSISTS MOSTLY
> OF GOING TO FUNERALS WHEN FOREIGN DIGNITARIES DIE

"Well, why don't you take the Quayle and insert the word Bush wherever it appears, and that's the crap I took for eight years. Wimp. Sycophant. Lapdog. Poop. Lightweight. Boob. Squirrel. Asshole. George Bush."

—President George Bush takes a moment to console his own VP

THEY JUST SAID "NO!"

"I do not choose to be buried until I am really dead."

—DANIEL WEBSTER, EXPLAINING WHY HE DECLINED THE
VICE-PRESIDENTIAL NOMINATION IN 1848

"I shall not, under any circumstances, consent to the employ-
ment of my name in connection with that office. Indeed
should I be nominated for it by the convention, I would most
assuredly decline. It is the very last office under the
Government I would desire to hold."

—JAMES BUCHANAN, DECLINING THE VICE-PRESIDENTIAL NOMINATION IN
1852. (WISE MOVE—HE WAS LATER ELECTED PRESIDENT IN 1856.)

"Ask him what he [Abraham Lincoln] thinks I have done to
deserve the punishment, at forty-six years of age, of being made
to sit as presiding officer over the Senate, to listen to debates,
more or less stupid, in which I can take no part nor say a word."

—MAJOR GENERAL BENJAMIN F. BUTLER, DECLINING THE
VICE-PRESIDENTIAL NOMINATION IN 1864

The (Second) Best America Has to Offer!

*O*ne party boss's perspective on why Nixon was chosen as Eisenhower's running mate: "We took Dick Nixon not because he was right wing or left wing—but because we were tired and he came from California."

• How underappreciated was Nixon by President Eisenhower? Near the end of Ike's last term, while Nixon was running his own presidential campaign, Ike was asked to give an example of one major idea of Nixon's that he as president had adopted. Ike's reply: "If you give me a week, I might think of one."

"How Dare You Call Me That?!"

*W*hen Al Gore was running for president in 1988 (four years before he accepted Bill Clinton's invitation to run as VP) he publically and vociferously rebuffed a heckler for shouting what he considered to be the ultimate insult.

Did the heckler insult Gore's mother? Make reference to the state of marriage of Gore's parents at the time of his birth? Insult his wife and children?

Nope. The insult to which Gore took such offense was that he had all the traits of a really good *vice* president.

Fifteen Minutes of Fame

*O*ccasionally a vice president who is otherwise un-noteworthy from a historical perspective will commit one act or coin one phrase that will live far longer than the name of the man himself. Such is the case of Vice President Thomas Marshall, who, while sitting through a long windy speech entitled "What This Country Needs" by a senator, commented to a nearby aide so everyone in the Senate could hear: "What this country needs is a really good five-cent cigar."

The Ultimate in Humiliation

*I*magine what it's like to be a vice president who has just lost a bid for the presidency: Because the VP is also the president of the Senate it is his job to count the votes of the electoral college before all members of Congress and to announce the name of the next president. Therefore, if you are VP and you have just lost the election, you have to suffer the ultimate humiliation of announcing the winner—your opponent—to Congress and God and everyone.

Just another way our founding fathers designed the job so as to give it to the VP in the shorts.

10

TAKE THIS JOB AND SHOVE IT!

*M*Y GOD! What is there in this place [the White House] that a man should ever want to get into it?" James Garfield once asked.

Beats me.

And before you assume Garfield was just suffering from a bad attitude problem or start asking yourself, *How bad could it really be?,* you should consider this: Garfield couldn't have been in office for very long before he came to this conclusion about the horrible job of the presidency . . . because less than four months after he was inaugurated someone shot him in the back.

"AND YOU CAN QUOTE ME ON THAT!"

JOHN ADAMS

"No man who ever held the office of president would congratulate a friend on obtaining it. He will make one man ungrateful, and a hundred men his enemies, for every office he can bestow."

"If I were to go over my life again, I would be a shoemaker rather than an American statesman."

THOMAS JEFFERSON

"Politics is such a torment that I would advise everyone I love not to mix with it."

"To myself personally, it brings nothing but unceasing drudgery and daily loss of friends."

Or was it George's smile they were admiring?

★ ★ ★

After his inauguration, John Adams commented to his wife that it really irked him that instead of looking at him, everyone in the crowd had their admiring eyes locked on Washington. He seemed to "enjoy a triumph over me," Adams told his wife. "Me thought I heard him say 'Ay, I am fairly out and you fairly in! See which of us will be happiest.'"

Take This Job and Shove It!

"I have the consolation . . . of having added nothing to my private fortune during my public service, and of retiring with hands as clean as they are empty."

(Jefferson died nearly penniless at the age of eighty-three.)

JOHN QUINCY ADAMS

"The four most miserable years of my life were my four years in the presidency."

ANDREW JACKSON

"I can say with truth that mine is a situation of dignified slavery."

MARTIN VAN BUREN

"As to the presidency, the two happiest days of my life were those of my entrance upon the office and my surrender of it."

JAMES POLK

"The office of president is generally esteemed a very high and dignified position. . . . I think the public would not so regard it if they could . . . observe the kind of people by whom I am often annoyed."

JAMES BUCHANAN

"If you are as happy, my dear sir, on entering the White House as I in leaving it and returning home, you are the happiest man in the country."

—BUCHANAN TO NEWLY ELECTED PRESIDENT ABRAHAM LINCOLN

ABRAHAM LINCOLN

"From my boyhood up, it was my ambition to be president. Now I am president of one part of this divided country, at least; but look at me! I wish I had never been born!"

"I am like the man who was tarred and feathered and ridden out of town on a rail. When they asked him how he felt about it, he said that if it were not for the honor of the thing, he would rather have walked."

RUTHERFORD B. HAYES

"My day is frittered away by the personal seeking of people, when I ought to be given to the great problems which concern the whole country. Four years of this kind of intellectual dissipation may cripple me for the remainder of my life."

"Being an errand boy to one hundred and fifty thousand people tires me so by night I am ready for bed instead of soirees."

Take This Job and Shove It!

JAMES GARFIELD

"My God! What is there in this place [the White House] that a
man should ever want to get into it?"

GROVER CLEVELAND

"The office of president has not, to me personally, a single allurement."

(Yet, after he lost in a bid for reelection in 1888 he ran again in 1892 and
won, making him the only president to serve nonconsecutive terms.)

THEODORE ROOSEVELT

"Ha ha! You are making up your Cabinet. I in a lighthearted way
have spent the morning testing the rifles for my African trip."

—TEDDY ROOSEVELT, IN A NOTE TO HIS FRIEND AND SUCCESSOR, WILLIAM HOWARD TAFT

WILLIAM HOWARD TAFT

"I have come to the conclusion that the major part of the work of a president is to increase
the gate receipts of expositions and fairs and bring the tourists into the town."

"I am glad to be going. This is the lonesomest place in the world."

—TAFT, AS HE LEFT THE WHITE HOUSE THE FINAL TIME

WARREN G. HARDING

"My God, this is a hell of a place for a man like me to be!"

"The White House is a prison. I can't get away from the men
who dog my footsteps. I am in jail."

HERBERT HOOVER

"This job is nothing but a twenty-ring circus—with a whole lot of bad actors."

"All the money in the world could not induce me to live over the last nine
months. The conditions we have experienced make this office a compound hell."

DWIGHT EISENHOWER

Unlike most of his fellow presidents, Ike didn't really want the job and was complaining
about it even before it was his.

"I furiously object to the word 'candidate'—I ain't and won't."

"I don't know why people are always nagging me to run for president. I think I've gotten too old."

"Those fools on the National Committee! Are they trying to perform the feat of electing a dead man?"

"I cannot conceive of any circumstance that could drag out of me permission to consider me for any political post from dogcatcher to Grand High Supreme King of the Universe."

"In the strongest language you can command you can state that I have no political ambitions at all. Make it even stronger than that if you can."

Once he had the job, Ike's chief complaint was that he could never get in a game of golf without being interrupted with phone calls from the State Department.

And the One That Got Away . . .

"I will not accept if nominated and will not serve if elected. . . . If forced to choose between the penitentiary and the White House for four years . . . I would say the penitentiary, thank you."

—CIVIL WAR GENERAL WILLIAM TECUMSEH SHERMAN IN 1884

CONCLUSION

I SPENT A YEAR READING, WRITING, AND THINKING ABOUT THIS BOOK.

When you write for a living you're constantly asked, "What are you working on?" And when asked during the past year I would describe this book in short detail. Almost uniformly, the response to my description would be one echoing a constant sentiment: that the men we elect as presidents today don't come close to measuring up to the standards of our forefathers. Conventional wisdom tells us, it seems, that our political ancestors were smarter, more honest, and more gentlemanly than politicians today.

I was always delighted to hear this response because it perfectly expressed what had been my anti-premise for the book since its date of conception.

In fact, this comment, which I heard over and over again, reminded me of a not particularly profound, but still very interesting, phenomenon of human nature: Members of a younger generation will very often assume members of older generations were boring and well behaved when they were at a similar age. One result of this misperception is that it always leads each successive generation to assume the sins and crimes and scandals of the present day are the worst the world has ever known. But hopefully, now that you've read this far, you've begun to look at history (at least as it pertains to our presidents) in a different light.

If you think about it, long before Watergate, Contragate, Travelgate, Nannygate, and Paulagate our presidents were lying, cheating, stealing, and womanizing—so the idea that our current crop of presidents don't "measure up" is both an inaccurate and silly one. I don't mean to say George Bush was a modern-day George Washington and Bill Clinton is a modern-day Thomas Jefferson. Rather, my point is that, of the forty-one men who have served as president of the United States, only Washington, Jefferson, Lincoln, Roosevelt, Roosevelt, and Truman have been of the caliber of Washington, Jefferson, Lincoln, Roosevelt, Roosevelt, and Truman. The rest have been (dare I say it?) mostly Fillmores, Pierces, Johnsons, Arthurs, and Clevelands. In other words: pretty darn average, pretty darn modest in the brains and talent departments, and . . . pretty darn forgettable.

Given the qualifiers above, what kind of feat is it to "measure up" to the standards of our forefathers anyway? Surely our current president and his last few predecessors have been at least as average and forgettable as most of the presidents of our past.

Which brings us to our true premise.

We began this book by suggesting that perhaps presidents ought not to be judged by their ability to govern or lead but by their ability to entertain—which is an interesting concept since the number and severity of a president's imbroglios seem to have nothing to do with his ability to govern and lead.

History will always remember Buchanan and Harding, for instance, as scandalous guys who made terrible presidents. In contrast, Jefferson and FDR will always be remembered as great presidents . . . who just happened to be scandalous as well.

And how will history remember Madison? McKinley? Harrison? Harrison? Or Hayes? The answer is history will barely remember them at all. These men were boring in life and boring in office—they failed to entertain. And when you've been elected to the office of president of the United States, there is no greater sign of failure and no worse slap in the face than to be remembered as a guy who did nothing that was worth being remembered for . . . or to get all the way to the White House but not be remembered at all.

With all this in mind, we offer you this quote a president once made to a friend about his predecessor: "If he was not the greatest president, he was the best actor of presidency we have ever had."

If we asked you to guess which president was being described, you'd be hard-pressed not to pick Ronald Reagan, of course.

But you'd be wrong.

The speaker was John Adams. And the president he was describing was none other than George Washington.

And that, dear reader, is entertainment.

★ ★ ★

It's impossible for us to draw this book to a close without saying something about media bias.

Trying to unravel the relationship between the presidency and the media (and you, the recipient of their final product) is sort of like trying to unravel the relationship between the chicken, the egg, and Einstein's relativity. It would be fun to figure out which came first, the chicken or the egg, but as Einstein's theory demonstrates, "first" is a matter of one's point of view.

Interestingly, news and politics work in a similar way. Case in point: I once had a conversation with the very conservative Oliver North in which he explained to me that he got a lot of his news from CNN even though he felt the network added a "left-wing" slant to their reporting. Not long afterward, I had a conversation with the very liberal Frank Zappa, who explained to me why he didn't like to watch too much CNN: "I find that their presentation is slanted and . . . so Republican, it's just smelly and it's suspicious."

So, which is it—the chicken or the egg? As Einstein might say, it all depends on your perspective.

Regardless of which direction you like to see your news slant, any attempts to view the contents of this book as an attack on (or support of) one particular political party or another will only be misguided. When it comes to presidential peccadilloes we just called 'em as we saw 'em and in true bipartisan spirit we did it without paying any attention to party lines.

Gregg Stebben
Carmel Valley, California
October 1997

APPENDIX A: WHAT'S IN A NAME?

WELL, IF YOU CONSIDER THAT IN 1958 a guy named John F. Kennedy, who worked in the stockroom of a razor factory, ran for the office of treasurer of Massachusetts and won on the strength of his name alone, you might begin to think there's more in a name than you presumed—especially if your name happens to be the same as Senator John Fitzgerald Kennedy's.

There's more than a little irony in this story, given that JFK's dad did essentially the same thing to help JFK get elected the first time he ran for office.

The year was 1946, and Kennedy was running for Congress. Joe Sr. was worried that a popular Boston city councilman, Joseph Russo, would get the upper hand in the race, so he cleverly went out and found another Joe Russo and paid him to put his name on the ballot.

In the end the two Joes split the Russo vote, and JFK won the election.

By the way, the JFK name not only bought the second Mr. Kennedy the election, it also allowed him to do it dirt cheap. In fact, his total campaign expenses amounted to about one hundred dollars—most of which was spent to throw an election-night party.

GERALD FORD

When Gerald Ford was born he was given the name Leslie Lynch King, but when his father died and his mother remarried, he was given his adoptive father's name: Gerald Ford. Therefore, punsters like to point out, Gerald Ford is the only president "born a King."

JOHN F. KENNEDY

JFK called his daughter Caroline "Buttons," and she called him "Silly Daddy." JFK called John Jr. "Foo Foo Head."

HARRY TRUMAN

Harry Truman called his wife, Bess, "The Boss" and his daughter, Margaret, "the one who bosses 'The Boss.'" The Secret Service called Truman, his wife, and his daughter "The Three Musketeers."

> "I was supposed to be named Harrison Shippe Truman, taking the middle name from my paternal grandfather. Others in the family wanted my middle name to be Solomon, taken from my maternal grandfather. But apparently no agreement could be reached and my name was recorded and stands simply as Harry S Truman."
>
> —HARRY TRUMAN*
>
> * NOTE THE ABSENCE OF A PERIOD AFTER HIS MIDDLE INITIAL; SINCE IT DOESN'T STAND FOR ANYTHING IT'S TECHNICALLY NOT AN INITIAL AND THEREFORE DOES NOT REQUIRE TRADITIONAL PUNCTUATION.

What's in a Name?

WOODROW WILSON

Folk singer Woodie Guthrie was named after Woodrow Wilson; his real name was Woodrow Wilson Guthrie.

ABE LINCOLN

Lincoln Logs were, in fact, named after Abraham Lincoln and the log cabin where Abe was born. Interestingly, Lincoln Logs were invented by John Lloyd Wright, the son of the famous architect Frank Lloyd Wright.

WILLIAM HENRY HARRISON

Boxer Jack Dempsey was named after President William Henry Harrison, believe it or not. Dempsey's real name was William Harrison Dempsey.

JAMES MONROE

The capital of the nation of Liberia is called Monrovia—in honor of President James Monroe.

RICHARD NIXON

Everyone's got a namesake and Richard Nixon's was King Richard the Lion-Hearted.

LBJ

It took good planning on the part of the Johnson family to get every member to have the same LBJ initials: Lyndon Baines, Lady Bird, Lynda Bird, and Luci Baines. As LBJ told it, when it came to monogramming it made things a whole lot cheaper.

ANDREW JACKSON

Andrew Jackson Borden, a mortician from Fall River, Massachusetts, had the honor of being named after the seventh president. But he is more famous for being murdered by his youngest daughter, Lizzie.

Appendix B: Presidential Firsts

YOU KNOW, IMPORTANT STUFF like which president was the first to wear a ponytail and which was the first to go snowboarding:

PRESIDENT:	**George Washington**
YEAR(S) IN OFFICE:	**1789-1797**

POLITICAL FIRST(S): George Washington became the first president to use a speech-writer when he asked Thomas Jefferson, James Madison, and Alexander Hamilton to help him draft his farewell address.

PRESIDENT:	**John Adams**
YEAR(S) IN OFFICE:	**1797-1801**

POLITICAL FIRST(S): John Adams was the first to serve as president and then lose in a reelection bid.

SOCIAL FIRST(S): John Adams and his family were the first to live in the White House. When it was time for the entire federal government to move its temporary quarters in Philadelphia to the new capitol in Washington, D.C., the entire enterprise—every document and file—fit into just seven packing cases.

PRESIDENT: Thomas Jefferson

YEAR(S) IN OFFICE: 1801-1809

POLITICAL FIRST(S): Thomas Jefferson was subpoenaed to testify in the treason trial of Aaron Burr, and he became the first president to invoke executive privilege.

SOCIAL FIRST(S): Thomas Jefferson was the first president to do away with bowing and to offer his hand for a handshake instead.

PRESIDENT: James Madison

YEAR(S) IN OFFICE: 1809-1817

POLITICAL FIRST(S): James Madison is the only president to have led troops into battle while he was in office. He did so while the British were trying to invade Washington during the War of 1812.

SOCIAL FIRST(S): James Madison was the first president to wear trousers while his successor, James Monroe, was the last president to wear knee breeches, buckled shoes, and three-cornered hats. Interestingly, Madison tended to push for change in government policy while Monroe generally liked to keep things status quo.

Presidential Firsts

PRESIDENT: **John Quincy Adams**
YEAR(S) IN OFFICE: **1825-1829**

TECHNOLOGIC FIRST(S): John Quincy Adams was the first president to ride on a train and the first to be photographed.

PRESIDENT: **Andrew Jackson**
YEAR(S) IN OFFICE: **1829-1837**

POLITICAL FIRST(S): Andrew Jackson was the first to win the presidency after losing in a first attempt. (The others were Nixon, Jefferson, William Henry Harrison, and Grover Cleveland.)

PRESIDENT: **Martin Van Buren**
YEAR(S) IN OFFICE: **1837-1841**

SOCIAL FIRST(S): Martin Van Buren was the first president to be born after the Declaration of Independence was signed and the first to be a United States citizen (all previous presidents were born British subjects).

PRESIDENT: **William Henry Harrison**
YEAR(S) IN OFFICE: **1841-1841**

SOCIAL FIRST(S): Not only was William Henry Harrison the first to die in office, but he also was the fastest to die—only thirty-one days after taking office.

PRESIDENT: **John Tyler**
YEAR(S) IN OFFICE: **1841-1845**

POLITICAL FIRST(S):
- Since President Harrison died after only thirty-one days in office, Tyler served the shortest term of any vice president.
- When William Henry Harrison died, John Tyler became the first VP to succeed to the office of president.
- He was the first to have a presidential veto overruled by Congress.

PRESIDENT: **Zachary Taylor**
YEAR(S) IN OFFICE: **1849-1850**

POLITICAL FIRST(S): Zachary Taylor was the first elected president who had never held a public office before. In fact, he had never even voted before—and he didn't even vote for himself.

Presidential Firsts

PRESIDENT: **Franklin Pierce**

YEAR(S) IN OFFICE: **1853-1857**

SOCIAL FIRST(S): Franklin Pierce was the first president to have a Christmas tree in the White House.

PRESIDENT: **James Buchanan**

YEAR(S) IN OFFICE: **1857-1861**

TECHNOLOGIC FIRST(S): James Buchanan was the first president ever to send or receive a transatlantic telegram.

SOCIAL FIRST(S): On the grand occasion of that first telegram, he exchanged greetings with the queen of England.

PRESIDENT: **Abraham Lincoln**

YEAR(S) IN OFFICE: **1861-1865**

TECHNOLOGIC FIRST(S): Abraham is the only president ever to receive a patent—#6469. His invention? A very complex device that used chambers of air to allow heavy ships to pass over shallow and dangerous waters.

SOCIAL FIRST(S): • Abraham Lincoln was the first president to have a beard. As the story goes, he was clean-shaven when he was nominated but decided to grow a beard after he got a letter from a little girl named Grace Bedell who wrote [sic]:

I have got 4 brothers and part of them will vote for you any way and if you let your whiskers grow I will try and get the rest of them to vote for you. You would look a great deal better for your face is so thin. All the ladies like whiskers and they would tease their husband's to vote for you and then you would be president.

Lincoln did as she suggested and then stopped his campaign train when it passed through her hometown. When Grace and her family joined the crowd assembled around Lincoln, he called her up to the front, kissed her, and said, "You see, I let these whiskers grow for you, Grace."

- The first child to die in the White House was Abraham Lincoln's twelve-year-old son, Willie.

PRESIDENT:	**Rutherford B. Hayes**
YEAR(S) IN OFFICE:	**1877-1881**

TECHNOLOGIC FIRST(S): Rutherford B. Hayes was the first president to have a typewriter. He also had the first telephone installed in the White House.

PRESIDENT:	**Chester Alan Arthur**
YEAR(S) IN OFFICE:	**1881-1885**

SOCIAL FIRST(S): Chester A. Arthur was the first president to smoke cigarettes.

Presidential Firsts

PRESIDENT: Grover Cleveland
YEAR(S) IN OFFICE: 1885-1889, 1893-1897

SOCIAL FIRST(S): Grover Cleveland was the first and only president to get married in the White House.

PRESIDENT: Benjamin Harrison
YEAR(S) IN OFFICE: 1889-1893

TECHNOLOGIC FIRST(S): Benjamin Harrison was the first president to have electricity in the White House.

PRESIDENT: William McKinley
YEAR(S) IN OFFICE: 1897-1901

TECHNOLOGIC FIRST(S): William McKinley was the first to use the telephone as part of his campaign strategy and the first to ride in a self-propelled vehicle—the electric ambulance that took him to the hospital after he had been shot.

PRESIDENT: Teddy Roosevelt

YEAR(S) IN OFFICE: 1901-1909

POLITICAL FIRST(S):
- Teddy Roosevelt was the first vice president to succeed to the presidency and then win the office in an election on his own. He was also the youngest man ever to serve as president—when McKinley died—although JFK was the youngest man ever elected.
- When Teddy Roosevelt made a trip to Panama to check on progress of the Panama Canal, it was the first time a president had ever left the country while in office.
- The first Jewish cabinet member, Oscar Straus, was appointed by Teddy Roosevelt. He was the head of the newly formed Department of Commerce and Labor.

TECHNOLOGIC FIRST(S): Teddy Roosevelt was the first president to ride in a car, go underwater in a submarine, and fly in a plane, although the plane trip was after he left office. His sub ride was in the *U.S.S. Plunger* and lasted about an hour. His airplane trip was at the St. Louis Aviation Field in a plane built by the Wright brothers. During the course of the trip, which lasted four minutes, the average cruising altitude was fifty feet.

Presidential Firsts

In spite of the fact that TR was the first president to experience advanced modes of transportation, he once blew up at his twenty-two-year-old daughter, Alice, and shouted, "The Roosevelts will remain a horse family!" when she suggested she'd like to travel by car once in a while.

SOCIAL FIRST(S):
- TR was the first to invite an African American to the White House for dinner. His guest was botanist Booker T. Washington.
- He was the first president to win the Nobel Peace Prize. (The only other president to win was Woodrow Wilson.)

PRESIDENT: William H. Taft

YEAR(S) IN OFFICE: 1909-1913

POLITICAL FIRST(S):
- William H. Taft was the first president required to pay federal income tax on his presidential salary.
- He is the only president to have served on the Supreme Court; he was eventually named chief justice.

SOCIAL FIRST(S): He was the first president to start the baseball season by throwing out the first pitch. Call it nepotism: After all, his brother was part owner of the Philadelphia Phillies. (It is also rumored that Taft is responsible for the seventh-inning stretch, which grew out of an incident where he tried to get out of his seat and his three-hundred-plus-pound frame got stuck.)

PRESIDENT: **Woodrow Wilson**

YEAR(S) IN OFFICE: **1913-1921**

TECHNOLOGIC FIRST(S):
- Wilson was the last president to ride to his inauguration in a horse-drawn carriage.
- He was also the first to cross the Atlantic.

SOCIAL FIRST(S): Woodrow Wilson was the first president to show a motion picture at the White House. Interestingly, the film was *Birth of a Nation*, which is considered by many film scholars to be one of the most important films in history because of its many technical innovations. (For instance, it was the first film to use night photography, tinting for dramatic effect, and close-up shots to reveal the intimate thoughts of a character.) On the other hand, because of its explicit and positive portrayal of the KKK, it is also the most banned film in American history.

PRESIDENT: **Warren G. Harding**

YEAR(S) IN OFFICE: **1921-1923**

TECHNOLOGIC FIRST(S): Warren G. Harding was the first president to own a radio and the first to make a speech over the radio waves. He was also the first to ride to his inauguration in a car and the first to know how to drive.

SOCIAL FIRST(S): When women got the right to vote, Harding was the first president they could elect.

Presidential Firsts

PRESIDENT: FDR

YEAR(S) IN OFFICE: 1933-1945

POLITICAL FIRST(S):
- The first woman to serve on a president's cabinet was Frances Perkins, appointed by FDR to the position of secretary of labor. She was once asked if she thought being a woman was in any way a handicap. "Only in climbing trees," she replied.
- Not only was FDR the first president to be elected for more than two terms (the tradition of seeking no more than two terms was unofficial, based on the precedence set by George Washington), but he was also the first candidate ever to win a presidential nomination after losing a bid for the vice presidency.

TECHNOLOGIC FIRST(S):
- Using a special switch that was set up at the White House, FDR was able to turn on the lights at Crosby Field in Cincinnati for the first night game in major league baseball history. (The Reds beat the Phillies 4-1.)
- The first bomb shelter and the first dishwasher were both installed in the White House during FDR's term in office.
- FDR was the first president ever to appear on television and the first president to fly in an airplane while in office (Teddy Roosevelt flew earlier, but not while in office).

PRESIDENT: **Harry Truman**
YEAR(S) IN OFFICE: **1945-1953**

POLITICAL FIRST(S): In 1948, sixty-four-year-old Harry Truman and seventy-year-old Alben Barkley were the oldest president-vice president team in history. Despite his age, Barkley campaigned in twenty-six states, delivering as many as fifteen speeches a day.

PRESIDENT: **Dwight D. Eisenhower**
YEAR(S) IN OFFICE: **1953-1961**

TECHNOLOGIC FIRST(S): • Dwight Eisenhower was the first president to appear on color TV.
• He was also the first president to go underwater in an atomic sub.
• He was the only president to have a pilot's license, and it was he who first used helicopters when making short trips on official business.

SOCIAL FIRST(S): Ike was the first president to hit a hole in one.

PRESIDENT: **JFK**
YEAR(S) IN OFFICE: **1961-1963**

POLITICAL FIRST(S): JFK won the presidency by a mere 120,000 votes out of a total of sixty-nine million ballots cast—the smallest margin ever. (This statistic actually tells only part of the story because it includes the votes cast for all minor-party candidates, as well as his Republican opponent, Richard Nixon. The number of votes that separated him from Nixon tells the true story: JFK did not win the votes of the majority of voters and could only claim one-tenth of 1 percent more popular votes than Nixon.

SOCIAL FIRST(S):
- JFK was the first Roman Catholic to be president. His one problem? It was difficult for him to find a priest to whom he could confess without the priest recognizing his voice.
- JFK was the first Boy Scout ever to become president.
- He was the first president to be born in the twentieth century.

> If you were born in 1953 or 1954, you were the first in the history of the nation to vote at age eighteen . . . and when you went to vote for the first time you had the choice of Richard Nixon or George McGovern.

PRESIDENT: LBJ

YEAR(S) IN OFFICE: 1963-1969

POLITICAL FIRST(S):
- LBJ appointed the first African American to a cabinet position. His name was Robert C. Weaver, and he was the head of the new Department of Housing and Urban Renewal.
- In the election of 1964 LBJ won 61 percent of the popular vote—more than any other president in history.

- LBJ was the first president to be present at his predecessor's assassination. He was also the first president to have his oath administered by a woman, the first to take his oath in an airplane, and the first to take the oath as his wife held the Bible. (His first presidential order after taking the oath was "Now, let's get airborne.")

TECHNOLOGIC FIRST(S): While in Australia, Johnson decided to fly back to Washington via Europe instead of over the Pacific, as he had come . . . and by doing so became the first president to circumnavigate the globe.

SOCIAL FIRST(S): When LBJ went to see the Washington Redskins play the Baltimore Colts in a preseason game in 1966, he became the first president to attend a pro football game while in office.

PRESIDENT:	**Richard Nixon**
YEAR(S) IN OFFICE:	**1969-1974**

POLITICAL FIRST(S): Richard Nixon is the only person ever elected twice to both the office of vice president and the office of president. He's also the only president ever to resign.

SOCIAL FIRST(S): Richard Nixon is the only president ever to have won an Emmy; he received the Best Spoken Word award for the album made from his televised interview with David Frost after leaving the presidency.

Presidential Firsts

PRESIDENT: Gerald Ford

YEAR(S) IN OFFICE: 1974-1977

POLITICAL FIRST(S): Gerald Ford was the first person to hold the office of vice president—and president—without being elected by the people; he was appointed vice president when Spiro Agnew resigned and then succeeded to the presidency when Nixon resigned.

PRESIDENT: Jimmy Carter

YEAR(S) IN OFFICE: 1977-1981

POLITICAL FIRST(S): Jimmy Carter appointed the first female African-American cabinet member, Patricia Roberts Harris. She was head of the Department of Housing and Urban Renewal.

SOCIAL FIRST(S): • Jimmy Carter was the first president born in a hospital.

• He is the first known president to go on record as having seen a UFO. The time was 1969, two years before he was elected governor of Georgia. The place: a Lion's Club meeting in Leary, Georgia. Jimmy and ten other club members spotted the object, which Jimmy described as "bright as the moon," "blueish at first, then reddish, luminious, not solid," and seeming to "move toward us from a distance, stop, move partially away, return, then depart." He also reported, in a detailed "sighting report" for the International UFO Bureau in Oklahoma City, that he had watched the object for ten to twelve minutes, that it produced no sound, and that it appeared to be about nine hundred yards away. "I'll never make fun of people who say they've seen unidentified objects in the sky," he was later heard to say. Jody Powell, Carter's press secretary, once quipped, "I would venture to say he [Carter] probably has seen stranger and more unexplainable things than that during his time in government."

PRESIDENT:	**Ronald Reagan**
YEAR(S) IN OFFICE:	**1981-1989**

POLITICAL FIRST(S):	The first Hispanic cabinet member was Lauro S. Cavazos, who was secretary of education under President Reagan.
SOCIAL FIRST(S):	Ronald Reagan was the first actor ever elected to the presidency, the oldest man ever elected to the office, the first to have been divorced, and the first to suffer from Alzheimer's disease.

PRESIDENT:	**George Bush**
YEAR(S) IN OFFICE:	**1989-1993**

TECHNOLOGIC FIRST(S):	George Bush was the first to use a personal computer.
SOCIAL FIRST(S):	George Bush was the first president to be asked by the press if he had ever committed adultery.

Presidential Firsts

PRESIDENT: Bill Clinton

YEAR(S) IN OFFICE: 1993-present

TECHNOLOGIC FIRST(S): Bill Clinton is the first president to have his administration represented on the Internet, although visiting www.billclinton.com will only link you to the Adult Chamber of Commerce, Eldorado Adult Novelties, Garlic Crabs Delivered World Wide, and Florida Tile & Marble Installations.

SOCIAL FIRST(S): • Bill Clinton is the first president ever to be both sued for sexual misconduct and forced to give a deposition while in office.
• He's the first Rhodes scholar ever elected president.

Appendix C: The George Washington Conspiracy

GEORGE WASHINGTON; FATHER OF OUR COUNTRY. America's first president. Right? Wrong.

Do the math. The thirteen original colonies of the United States of America proclaimed their independence in 1776. George Washington became president in 1789.

That leaves a gap of thirteen years—thirteen years when *someone* must have been running the country . . . right?

Right. And that first someone was a guy by the name of John Hanson—who won the job by a unanimous vote of Congress.

Hanson was then followed by Elias Boudinot, the second president of the United States. And Thomas Mifflin, the third president. Richard Henry Lee, the fourth. Nathan Gorman, the fifth. Arthur St. Clair, the sixth. Cyrus Griffin, the seventh. And George Washington, the eighth.

Pretty weird, huh?

It's George Washington and the Seven (Political) Dwarves

If seven different men really did serve as president before George Washington, why did we all learn in school that George was number one?

Because George was the first president to rule under the Constitution we follow today. His seven predecessors, on the other hand, all served as president under the *Articles of Confederation,* a sort of first-draft Constitution.

Many historians deny the legitimacy of Hanson's presidency because the Articles of Confederation only served to bring the thirteen colonies together into a sort of loose association or "league of friendship" called the Continental Congress.

According to the Articles of Confederation, states had the right to make their own decisions, and since states' rights were all the rage, there was no provision for a central or national government that would have the right to meddle in the states' affairs.

In fact, it wasn't until the passage of the Constitution in 1789 that a federal government was created.

The absence of a federal government, executive branch, or chief executive in the Articles of Confederation was no accident. It was all part of the plan: After all, the authors of the Articles were rebelling against the tyrannical and upper-handed rule of the king of England, so why would they create a new government that gave someone else the power to control their lives?

Unfortunately for John Hanson, this little glitch in our constitutional law has made it possible for some historians to say he was merely the president of the Continental Congress and not of the United States of America.

Confused?

Here's a quick time line of history that will make things a lot clearer . . . since you probably only heard a fraction of this in your high school civics class:

- June 11, 1776: The Articles of Confederation, which proposed that the original thirteen colonies form a loose federal government, were presented to the young Continental Congress.
- November 15, 1777: Congress ratified the Articles, but they were still not the law. That wouldn't happen until all thirteen colonies approved.
- 1777-81: Conflict! The citizens of Maryland felt that because the size of their territory was dwarfed by the sizes of Virginia and New York, they wouldn't get equal representation under the Articles of Confederation unless the two larger states ceded some of their land—thus giving Maryland equal footing in terms of size and representation.
- 1781: Finally! All thirteen colonies have signed the Articles of Confederation.
- November 5, 1781: John Hanson was elected "President of the United States in Congress Assembled" by a unanimous vote of Congress.
- 1787: The Constitution was drafted; it was ratified in 1788 and took effect in 1789.
- February 4, 1789: George Washington was the eighth man to be elected president by a unanimous vote of the electoral college.

"... *Powers and Duties, Unimaginable to the Founders*"

If it's fair to deny that John Hanson was our first president, then it's also fair to say most of the other men we recognize as having served as president (all those, say, from Washington to McKinley) weren't either. For as Edward S. Greenberg and Benjamin I. Page explain in their textbook *The Struggle for Democracy:*

> *Since Franklin Roosevelt's day, the American presidency has involved powers and duties, unimaginable to the Founders.*

Over time the presidency has evolved. As chief executive, George Washington never had to worry about terrorism, nuclear disarmament, pollution, overpopulation, homelessness, or Internet pornography, or a host of things that must drive modern presidents mad. Was he any less of a president because of it?

JOHN HANSON: WAS HE . . . OR WASN'T HE?

So, who are you going to believe? Some history professor who wears tweed, smokes a pipe, and gets paid to put college freshmen to sleep? Or are you going to put your money on a couple of guys who were actually there?

> **"Mr. President. I feel very sensibly the favorable declaration of Congress expressed by your Excellency."**
>
> —GEORGE WASHINGTON TO JOHN HANSON, A FEW WEEKS AFTER HANSON WAS ELECTED PRESIDENT

> **"[George] Washington accepts every condition, law, rule and authority, under the Great Seal and the first President of the United States, John Hanson."**
>
> —THOMAS JEFFERSON, WHILE SERVING AS GEORGE WASHINGTON'S SECRETARY OF STATE

Conspiracy Theorists Wanted: Please Apply Within

Here's the thing about John Hanson's tenure in office that is impossible to fathom: If George Washington and Thomas Jefferson knew John Hanson was the first president of the United States, how come the rest of us have never heard of him before?

Could it be . . . a conspiracy?

In 1932 Seymour Wemyss Smith wrote a book called *John Hanson, Our First President.* In the preface Hal F. Lee reported that:

> *The only references to John Hanson in the card indices of the New York Public Library mention two articles [both of which Smith wrote] . . . and the* Encyclopaedia Britannica *took cognizance of Hanson for the first time in its Fourteenth Edition, dated 1929, having failed even to mention his*

What Do You Think?

★ ★ ★

Okay, it's true. Lee sounds a bit like a nut. We thought so too—until we cracked open a copy of *Encyclopaedia Britannica's* 1954 Great Books series to read the Articles of Confederation verbatim. Everything looked fine until we got to the end . . . where you would expect to see the names of the forty-eight men—which included the likes of Hanson, of course, Samuel Adams, and John Hancock—who signed the Articles into law. Instead we found just one name printed there: George Washington.

George, however, was not one of the forty-eight who signed the Articles of Confederation.

name in former editions. . . . To George Washington seven pages of the Encyclopedia are justly devoted—to John Hanson but fourteen brief lines.

Furthermore, Lee writes:

Washington was a prolific writer. For a score of years he made almost daily entries in his diary. It is odd that Washington's diary is so complete up to the date of the election of John Hanson as our first President, Nov. 5, 1781, and that no further entries can be found until almost a year after Hanson's death? Washington knew Hanson well. It is probable that he commented at length upon Hanson's administration. But his diary covering this period is missing.

Or Was John Hanson Just Too Darn Boring?

If only John Hanson had lived long enough to read this book. He would have known: It's not what you do as president that counts—it's how much entertainment you provide and how much coverage in the press you get.

As Seymour Wemyss saw it:

Legends concerning Washington became national epics. He was not only "father of his country." He chopped down a cherry tree and could not tell a lie. He threw a dollar across the Potomac. He was "first in war, first in peace and first in the hearts of his countrymen." Of such stories are heroes made. Did John Hanson lack an efficient publicity department? Was he too absorbed in his job to think of what we today call "public relations"?

Yup. Too absorbed.

And it's kind of sad too. Because even though he was a terrible president when it came to doing things to ensure his immortality and his place in history, when it was time to take care of the unimportant stuff—like running the country—Hanson did an admirable job. Especially when you consider that according to the Articles of Confederation he was limited to a term of just one year.

A YEAR IN THE LIFE OF OUR FIRST PRESIDENT

John Hanson took office just as the Revolutionary War ended, and he ordered all foreign troops off U.S. soil—making it the first time in almost two hundred years that all thirteen colonies were free of foreign armies. He took the United States from a wartime nation following the Revolutionary War to a nation at peace. This meant that he had to drastically reduce the size of the U.S. Army without causing a mutiny, a difficult task considering that the new government had no money to pay existing soldiers for the work they had already done.

When those same unpaid soldiers threatened to take over the new government by force, every single member of the Continental Congress left . . . except Hanson. Instead he stood tall, and as the lone representative of the new United States government he negotiated a peaceful settlement.

He created the Treasury Department, the Department of Foreign Affairs, and the position of secretary of war. He also chartered a national bank, initiated a postal service, and established the first consular service. He was even, by some accounts, the one to declare the fourth Thursday of every November a national holiday: Thanksgiving.

POOR JOHN HANSON—ALL THE WORK, NONE OF THE GLORY

While writing this, your authors found themselves feeling kind of bad for John Hanson.

So bad, in fact, that as soon as we're finished here we're going to write to both our representatives in Congress and the president and demand that John Hanson be recognized and given his due. If you're smart, you'll do the same. After all, if we work together and successfully convince our leaders in Washington to pass a law that says schools must teach about the "real" first president of the United States—in addition to whatever they already have to say about George Washington—we'll all accrue great benefit from our efforts.

First, we'll get the joy and satisfaction of seeing our government at work. Second, we'll each get an opportunity to experience the thrill of knowing our voices count.

And finally, there's the most important reason we should join together and undertake this important project: If we're successful, we'll all get another day off from work every year. After all, we're not going to be foolish enough to insist that the federal government crown this guy as "first president of the United States" without also insisting that they make his birthday (April 3) a national holiday too.

BUT WAIT A MINUTE!

Astute readers may have noticed that in spite of all that has been said here about John Hanson, he probably wasn't the first president of the United States either . . . since the Declaration of Independence was signed in 1776 and Hanson didn't take office until 1781.

So who was in charge before Hanson? For the answer to that question and many others that are sure to arise, we direct you to *The Patriot's Handbook,* by Dr. George Grant. Even more a purist than the two of us, Grant says we had a president as early as 1774, when the Continental Congress first began to meet. Grant's list of presidents, therefore, begins with Peyton Randolph of Virginia.

Randolph served as the president of the first Continental Congress from September 5 to October 21, 1774. But while Grant presents a convincing case for Randolph's presidency, Hanson still gets our vote. After all, you'll recall Hanson was the guy Washington called "Mr. President" and whom Jefferson called "the first President of the United States." And how can you argue with that?

Acknowledgments

ONE COLD WINTER NIGHT in 1995 I took my girlfriend Jody to the movies to see a schmaltzy love story called *The American President.* At the end of the show two very significant events occurred. First, as the credits rolled I had the idea for this book. Second, as I got up to leave, Jody pulled me back down into my seat, kissed me, and asked me—a solidly confirmed thirty-four-year-old bachelor—if I wouldn't like to be her husband someday.

As good an idea as I thought this book was, I thought Jody's idea was even better. And I'm no longer a bachelor, solidly confirmed or otherwise. Meanwhile, I'm happy to report that this book—and everything else in my life—is demonstrably better for the addition of the ever-smiling, ever-loving Jody Stebben.

When it comes to the book, lots of other people helped. Cara Lieb read the first draft, looked me in the eye, and told me quite honestly that it stank; Robert Walters took the time to read a later draft and insisted I let him keep reading (which I took as a good sign); Victor, Steve, Susan, and the rest of the staff of the Monterey Public Library came to my aid and helped me locate and check out several hundred library books at a time.

Lizz McKeon introduced me to a great editor and publisher, Ron Pitkin of Cumberland House Publishing. Ron Montana introduced me to my agent, Laurie Harper of the Sebastian Agency, who negotiated a contract that left both Ron Pitkin and me smiling. When the book was complete, Leslie Peterson of Cumberland House did a great job of turning my "writing style" into decipherable English. My thanks to them all. And it is all due to the brilliance of

PR-wiz Glenn Schwartz that I met Jim Morris, who has been a tremendous inspiration and resource.

Other folks: my now-departed grandmother, Ann Stebben; my brother, Marty; my cousin, Jackie Diamond; Dale Forbes, who helped me come up with the title; Barbara Fairchild of *Bon Appétit,* Dave Zinzencko of *Men's Health,* and Jeff Csatari of *Verge,* who helped finance the project by continuing to give me work in their magazines; and Paul Sledzik of the National Museum of Health and Medicine in Washington, D.C., who aided me in my now-obsessive search for the pistol used to assassinate President Garfield (which has been missing for almost forty-five years). Many others—like Dr. Richard Westbrook, Judy Tatelbaum, Janis Lonnquist, Linda Smith, Joanne Gruber, Carole Barrett, Louise Bullock, Jennifer Lyons, Wes Hester, Tom Biggs, Randy Rapp, Bill O'Connell, Cynthia Heller, Heather Bach, Larry Goldberg, Bridget Ward, Dee Bestill and Charles Hamilton—were always there when I called for help. And a bit belatedly, I thank my good friend Denis Boyles for showing me the ropes.

Finally, darn it, I've got to thank Rob Reiner, Michael Douglas, and Annette Bening for making that sappy little movie *The American President.* As silly as this may sound, things just haven't been the same around here since I saw it.

—G. S.

★ ★ ★

*C*ALL ME ARROGANT, but I want to thank the forty-one (or forty-eight; see Appendix C) men who have selflessly served as president of the United States. We never could have done it without you.

Acknowledgments

I also want to thank Glenn Schwartz, my longtime publicist, for his never-flagging support and for landing me this gig; Joe Lauer, who provided me with years of guidance as my personal manager; and my father, Harvey Morris, who put up with me through my deformative years. It was he who inspired me (unwittingly, of course) to pursue a career of questioning authority.

And I want to thank you, the reader. Over the years you could have thrown your votes away on guys who were actually qualified for the job of president. You could have picked boring guys to lead you—guys whose names we wouldn't even remember anymore. But instead you always made the wise choice and voted for the guys you knew would keep you laughing. And in so doing you make it possible for me to have a job.

Finally, I want to single out and thank Richard Nixon. Here was a guy with absolutely no sense of humor, as far as I could tell as a kid. Yet he knew that if he couldn't entertain us— the troops at home in the living rooms and barcaloungers of America—if he couldn't make us laugh, it would all be over for him. So he did the only logical thing: He appeared on *Rowan & Martin's Laugh-In* as a guest, popped his head through his door in the wall at the end of the show just like Lily Tomlin did every week, and said with all the feeling he could muster: "Sock it to me!"

Richard Nixon, that night you changed my life. You helped make me what I am today: a guy who gets to "act" as goofy as a president and make people laugh—and still pay his bills. Thank you. God bless you. And God bless the United States of America.

—J. M.

About the Authors

Gregg Stebben is the author of several books, including the Man's Life series. He has written for *Esquire, Bon Appétit, Men's Health,* and *TV Guide* and as a journalist has interviewed public figures ranging from President Clinton to Mikhail Gorbachev to O. J. Simpson. He lives in Carmel Valley, California.

★ ★ ★

Jim Morris, who has been called "a living political cartoon," is a political impressionist who specializes in poking fun at presidents and other public figures. Morris appears regularly in such broadcasts as *Larry King Live, Politically Incorrect, Good Morning America, The Today Show, Comic Relief, The Tonight Show,* and *Crossfire.* He has been featured at the White House and Washington Correspondents' Dinner, and has entertained in the Oval Office. He lives near Dallas, Texas.